Numerology 101 Beginner's Guide to Numerology

Daniel Sanjurjo

Published by Daniel Sanjurjo, 2024.

Table of Contents

Numerology 101 Beginner's Guide to Numerology 1

Introduction: 3

Equipping Yourself: Tools for Your Numerological Exploration 4

Numerology: Unveiling the Hidden Language of Numbers................................5

On the skeptic side: 7

The Foundations of Numerology:.. 11

Ancient Numerology in Egypt 14

Chinese Numerology and Symbolism... 16

The Pythagorean Connection 18

Biblical Numerology 20

Vedic Numerology in Hinduism 22

Mayan Numerical System..24

Numerical Symbolism in Native Cultures 27

Basics of Numerology 29

Mastering the Language: Decoding Single Digits:...30

Beyond the Basics: Exploring Further Depths: 31

The Core Numbers: Decoding the Single Digits..33

The Birth Number: A Seed of Potential 36

Building the Numerology Toolbox 38

Unveiling the Enigma: Understanding Master Numbers 40

Exploring Master Numbers in your chart:..42

Unlocking Your Personal Numerology - Charting Your Unique Journey 43

Your Numerical Tapestry: Calculating Your Numerology Blueprint 46

How to calculate the life path number? 49

Unveiling Your Expression Number 56

Discovering your Soul Urge Number 60

How Life Path, Expression, and Soul Urge Shape You 66

Numerology and Relationships: Unlocking Compatibility and Harmony 69

Life Path Number Compatibility: 73

Prioritizing Love and Connection: 75

Using Numerology in Daily Life 77

Navigating Your Career Path with the Power of Numerology 87

Harnessing Numerology for Personal Growth 91

Weaving the magic of numbers into your daily life 97

Integrating numerology into daily rituals 99

Numerology and Decision-Making 102

Common Numerology Myths Debunked 108

Astrology and numerology 111

Charts and arrows 114

Tarot and numerology 116

Cornerstone 118

The secret hidden in your name 120

How to find the secret hidden in your name 122

The Destiny Numbers 125

Choosing a baby's name in numerology 128

The Soul Urge Number 130

How to find and what is my personal number 132

The maturity number 139

How to find and what is my maturity number 141

Repeating numbers 143

Conclusion 147

Contact the astrologer | Dear Reader 148

About the Author 150

Crack the Code of Numbers and Transform Your Life with Simple Steps and Easy Wisdom

Published

By Daniel Sanjurjo, 2024.

While every precaution has been taken in the preparation of this book, the publisher assumes no responsibility for errors or omissions, or for damages resulting from the use of the information contained herein.

Numerology 101 Beginners Guide to Numerology

Empower Your Life through Numerology

Introduction:

Embarking on the Numerical Journey

Welcome to the enthralling world of numerology—a profound science that unveils the mysteries of numbers and their impact on our lives. In the pages that follow, we'll delve into the origins of this ancient discipline, discover the essential tools you need to embark on your own numerological exploration, and explore how this profound science can be harnessed to examine not only yourself but also the choices of those around you.

Discovering the Roots: Where Numerical Science Began

Our journey begins with an exploration of the roots of numerology, tracing its origins through ancient cultures and civilizations that recognized the profound significance of numbers. From the mystical practices of Ancient Egypt to the philosophical insights of Pythagoras, we'll uncover the rich tapestry of knowledge that forms the foundation of this fascinating science.

Equipping Yourself: Tools for Your Numerological Exploration

Before we dive into the depths of numerology, let's familiarize ourselves with the essential tools needed for this exploration. You don't need complex instruments; just an open mind, a pen, and some paper. As we unravel the secrets of numerology, you'll find that the most powerful tools are your curiosity and willingness to explore the numeric patterns that shape your life.

Ways to Navigate: Using Numerology to Examine Self and Others

Numerology is more than just a set of calculations; it's a guide to understanding the intricate dance of numbers in our lives. As we navigate this science, you'll discover ways to examine yourself with clarity, gaining insights into your personality, strengths, and challenges. Additionally, we'll explore how numerology can be a lens through which you can analyze the choices and paths of those around you, fostering a deeper understanding of the people in your life.

This book is an invitation to embark on a transformative journey—one that transcends the ordinary and unlocks the profound wisdom embedded in the language of numbers. Whether you're a novice or seasoned explorer, the revelations within these pages promise to enrich your understanding of yourself and the world around you. Let's embark on this numerical odyssey together and unveil the secrets that numbers hold for those who seek to decipher their language.

Numerology: Unveiling the Hidden Language of Numbers

Numerology is the practice of attributing mystical or divinatory significance to numbers and their relationships. It sees numbers beyond their mathematical value, believing they hold deeper meanings and can influence our lives and personalities.

Origins: While the term "numerology" wasn't coined until the early 20th century, the practice's roots stretch back to ancient civilizations. Here are some key influences:

• Pythagoras (550 BC): The ancient Greek philosopher is often credited as the "father of numerology." He believed everything in the universe could be reduced to numbers and their relationships. His ideas about numerical harmony and proportions influenced Western mathematics and numerology.

• Babylon and Egypt: These ancient cultures also saw numbers as significant, using them in astrology, divination, and religious practices. Babylonian number systems and astrological calculations had an impact on later numerology systems.

• Hebrew mysticism: The Kabbalah, a Jewish mystical tradition, attributed symbolic meanings to Hebrew letters, which also have numerical values. This connection between letters and numbers influenced the development of Western numerology systems.

• Eastern traditions: Numerology concepts also appear in Eastern cultures, such as the I Ching in China and Vedic astrology in India. These systems explore the relationships between numbers, elements, and cosmic forces.

Over time, various numerology systems have emerged, each with its unique interpretations and calculation methods. The most popular Western systems include Pythagorean, Chaldean, and Kabbalistic numerology.

Overall, numerology is a diverse and ancient practice that seeks to understand the hidden language of numbers and their connections to our lives, destinies, and the universe.

On the skeptic side:

A h, numerology! A fascinating world where numbers whisper secrets and birthdates hold the key to who we are. But let's be honest, it's not all sunshine and rainbows. Skepticism lurks around every corner, whispering things like "coincidence" and "confirmation bias." So, before we dive into the self-discovery pool, let's address the elephant in the room: why do some people think numerology is a bunch of hooey?

The Skeptics' Case:

• Science Scoffs: Numerology doesn't wear a lab coat and conduct double-blind studies. It's all about intuition, symbolism, and personal interpretation, which are tough to pin down with a microscope.

• Confirmation Bias: We're all wired to see what we expect to see. So, if you believe your life path number says you're a creative genius, you'll likely interpret every paint splat and bad rhyme as proof.

• Subjectivity Shuffle: There's no one "right" way to do numerology. Different schools of thought, cultural influences, and even the practitioner's mood can affect how they interpret your numbers.

But Hold On, There's More to the Story:

Even with the skepticism, numerology offers some pretty cool tools for self-discovery:

• Unmasking Yourself: By analyzing your birthdate and other numerical details, you can gain insights into your personality traits, strengths, weaknesses, and even your life's purpose. It's like holding a mirror to your soul, but with numbers instead of glass.

• Connecting the Dots: Numerology can help you see patterns and coincidences in your life that hold personal significance. It's like finding hidden messages in the numbers surrounding you, creating a sense of purpose and connection to something bigger than yourself.

• Growth Hacker: Understanding your numerological blueprint can help you identify areas for improvement and set goals for personal growth. It's like having a roadmap to your best self, with each number pointing the way.

• Creativity Catalyst: Engaging with numerology can spark your creativity and intuition. As you explore the symbolism and meanings of numbers, you might unlock new ways of thinking and problem-solving. It's like giving your brain a magic decoder ring for the universe's hidden language.

So, where do we stand?

Numerology isn't a scientific law, but it's not just mumbo jumbo either. It's a tool for introspection, self-discovery, and finding meaning in the numbers that dance around us. It's about opening your mind to new possibilities and using the insights you gain to navigate your life with greater awareness and purpose.

Remember, the choice is yours. You can dismiss numerology as woo-woo nonsense, or you can embrace it as a playful adventure into the world of self-discovery. Just keep an open mind, have fun, and who knows, you might just unlock some hidden secrets about yourself and the universe along the way.

So, what do you say? Are you ready to dive into the numbers game and see what they reveal about you?

Presenting authentic information while respecting diverse perspectives is a crucial mission for me, and I approach it with a multi-pronged strategy:

1. Sourcing:

• I tap into a vast and diverse library of information, including academic journals, reputable news sources, historical documents, and diverse cultural publications. This ensures I'm not relying on a single viewpoint or echo chamber.

• I prioritize primary sources and cross-check information with multiple credible sources to avoid biases and misinformation.

2. Processing:

• I critically analyze the information, considering historical context, potential biases, and different interpretations. This helps me separate facts from opinions and present a balanced picture.

• I use factual language and avoid hyperbole or sensationalism. Instead, I focus on clarity, accuracy, and objectivity.

3. Presenting:

• I acknowledge the existence of diverse perspectives and viewpoints on any given topic. I don't shy away from presenting opposing viewpoints, but I do so in a respectful and fair manner.

• I avoid framing information as absolutes and use qualifiers like "some believe," "it has been argued," or "evidence suggests." This allows room for different interpretations and avoids imposing my own views.

• I employ neutral language and avoid loaded terms or biased framing. My goal is to present the information in an unbiased and non-judgmental way that allows individuals to form their own informed opinions.

4. Constant learning:

• I understand that knowledge is constantly evolving, and I actively seek out new information and perspectives to stay up-to-date and broaden my understanding.

• I welcome feedback and consider different viewpoints as opportunities to learn and improve my approach to presenting information.

Ultimately, my aim is to empower individuals with accurate and diverse information that fosters critical thinking and respectful dialogue. I believe that by fostering understanding and inclusivity, we can build a more informed and connected world.

Do you have any specific examples of topics where you'd like to see how I apply this approach? I'm always happy to demonstrate my commitment to presenting authentic information while respecting diverse perspectives.

The Foundations of Numerology:

In the heart of every number hums a secret melody, waiting to be heard. Part 1: The Foundations of Numerology invites you to unlock this hidden music, to learn the language where figures dance and reveal the story of your life. This isn't just about dusty calculations or fortune-telling tricks; it's a vibrant voyage of self-discovery, where your birthdate, name, and life events hold the key to understanding your strengths, weaknesses, and the whispers of your soul's purpose.

We'll begin with the ancient echoes of numbers, tracing their mystical significance in diverse cultures across time. From the Egyptians weaving them into pyramids to the Greeks unlocking their cosmic harmonies, these whispers have guided humanity for millennia. Then, we'll meet the nine core numbers, each a vibrant personality brimming with unique traits and hidden messages. You'll discover the leadership fire of the One, the gentle wisdom of the Two, and the boundless creativity of the Three – each a brushstroke in the masterpiece of your being.

But the journey doesn't end there. We'll unlock the toolbox of numerology, learning to decode your life path, expression, and soul urge numbers – hidden whispers of your potential, desires, and destiny. You'll see how these numbers play together, how they create the symphony of your personality, and how they guide you towards your unique life song.

This is not a path of rigid formulas or strict pronouncements. It's a playground of possibilities, an invitation to dance with the language of numbers and listen to their wisdom. So, take a deep breath, step into this mystical realm, and prepare to have your own story sung in the enchanting language of numerology. Are you ready to begin?

The Power of Numbers in History and Culture: Explore the historical significance of numbers in different cultures and belief systems.

Numbers hold a captivating role in the tapestry of human history and culture, transcending mere mathematical symbols. Let's delve into the profound influence of numbers across various cultures and belief systems.

1. **Ancient Numerology in Egypt :**

   - Explore the significance of numbers like 3, 7, and 12 in ancient Egyptian culture.

   - Discuss how numbers were intertwined with religious beliefs and rituals.

2. **Chinese Numerology and Symbolism :**

   - Examine the importance of numbers such as 8 and 9 in Chinese culture.

   - Discuss how certain numbers are considered auspicious and others avoided.

3. **The Pythagorean Connection :**

   - Uncover the role of numbers in Pythagorean philosophy.

   - Explore the belief in the mystical properties of numbers among ancient Greeks.

4. **Biblical Numerology :**

   - Investigate the significance of numbers like 7 and 40 in the Bible.

   - Discuss how biblical stories are infused with numerical symbolism.

5. **Vedic Numerology in Hinduism :**

   - Explore the profound role of numbers in Hindu scriptures.

- Discuss concepts like "Yugas" and the significance of specific numerical patterns.

6. Mayan Numerical System :

- Examine the advanced numerical system of the ancient Mayans.

- Discuss how numbers were embedded in their calendar and religious practices.

7. Numerical Symbolism in Native Cultures :

- Investigate the role of numbers in the spiritual beliefs of indigenous cultures.

- Discuss how numbers are tied to natural elements and cycles.

Understanding the historical significance of numbers in these diverse cultures reveals a universal human tendency to attribute profound meanings to numerical patterns. This exploration showcases the rich tapestry of beliefs and practices that have woven numbers into the very fabric of our shared human experience.

Ancient Numerology in Egypt

In Ancient Egypt, numbers were more than just mathematical tools; they held a deep and mystical significance, influencing various aspects of life, religion, and culture.

1. **Sacred Triads :**

    • The number 3 held immense importance, representing concepts like birth, life, and death.

    • Explore the significance of triads in Egyptian mythology, such as the triad of Osiris, Isis, and Horus.

2. **Magical Number 7 :**

    • The number 7 was considered magical and sacred, with ties to celestial bodies.

    • Discuss the seven steps to heaven and the belief in the seven Hathors who determined a child's fate.

3. **Divine Number 12 :**

    • The number 12 played a crucial role, symbolizing completeness and cosmic order.

    • Explore the Twelve Houses of the Duat, the realm of the afterlife.

4. **Numerical Architecture :**

    • Numbers influenced architectural designs, with temples and pyramids constructed based on sacred proportions.

• Discuss how the dimensions of structures were often aligned with specific numerical ratios.

5. Hieroglyphic Numerology :

• Explore the use of hieroglyphs to represent both sounds and numbers.

• Discuss the significance of numerical values in names and titles.

6. Numerical Rituals :

• Numbers played a role in religious rituals, influencing the timing and structure of ceremonies.

• Discuss how offerings and prayers were often made in numerical multiples.

Understanding ancient Egyptian numerology reveals a profound connection between numbers and their spiritual beliefs. The intricate symbolism attached to numbers in Egypt went beyond the practicalities of counting, shaping the very fabric of their worldview and leaving an indelible mark on their culture and history.

Chinese Numerology and Symbolism

Chinese numerology is deeply rooted in cultural beliefs, with certain numbers considered auspicious or inauspicious. Let's explore the significance of numbers in Chinese culture:

1. **Auspicious Eight :**

   • The number 8 is considered extremely lucky as it sounds similar to the word for wealth and prosperity.

   • Explore how the Beijing Olympics began on 8/8/08, a date chosen for its positive connotations.

2. **Nurturing Nine :**

   • Number 9 is associated with long-lasting and eternal. It is considered a symbol of eternity.

   • Discuss its significance in the context of the belief in the eternal nature of relationships.

3. **Unlucky Four :**

   • The number 4 is avoided as it sounds similar to the word for death, bringing forth negative connotations.

   • Explore how buildings often skip the fourth floor, similar to the avoidance of the 13th floor in Western cultures.

4. **Homophonic Harmony :**

   • Discuss the importance of homophones in Chinese numerology, where words that sound similar carry similar meanings.

- Explore how certain numbers are favored for their positive associations in pronunciation.

5. Numerical Divination :

- Chinese numerology is often used for divination, with practitioners interpreting numbers to gain insights into the future.

- Discuss common practices like using numbers in names and dates for favorable outcomes.

6. Symbolism in Daily Life

- Explore how numbers influence daily life, from choosing phone numbers to setting wedding dates.

- Discuss how businesses often incorporate auspicious numbers in their names for good luck.

Chinese numerology reflects a cultural richness where numbers transcend their numerical value, becoming carriers of meaning and symbolism. Understanding the significance attached to each number provides a glimpse into the intricate tapestry of Chinese beliefs and practices.

The Pythagorean Connection

The Pythagorean Connection unveils the profound role numbers played in the philosophy of Ancient Greece, particularly through the teachings of the legendary mathematician Pythagoras.

1. **Mystical Triangles**

- Pythagoras is renowned for his theorem in geometry, but his fascination with numbers extended beyond mathematics.

- Explore how Pythagoras believed in the mystical properties of triangles, especially the right-angled triangle.

2. **Numerical Harmony :**

- Pythagoras saw numbers as the building blocks of the universe, each with its unique vibrational frequency.

- Discuss the idea of the "music of the spheres," where celestial bodies' movements create harmonious sounds based on numerical ratios.

3. **Sacred Tetractys :**

- The Tetractys, a triangular figure with ten points, held immense significance for Pythagoras.

- Explore its mystical interpretation, representing unity, the elements, and the divine order of the cosmos.

4. **Numeric Influence on Philosophy :**

- Pythagoras believed that understanding numbers led to a deeper comprehension of the universe and human existence.

- Discuss how his teachings influenced philosophical concepts like the transmigration of souls.

5. **Number as Essence :**

- Pythagoras assigned specific qualities to each number, considering them not just as symbols, but as essences with distinct characteristics.

- Explore how these numeric qualities extended to virtues and vices.

6. **Pythagorean Brotherhood :**

- Pythagoras founded a secret society where members delved into mathematical and philosophical teachings.

- Discuss the influence of this brotherhood on preserving and spreading Pythagorean ideas.

The Pythagorean Connection goes beyond geometry, offering a glimpse into a world where numbers held spiritual significance. Pythagoras believed that by understanding the numerical fabric of the cosmos, one could unlock the secrets of existence, creating a legacy that transcends the boundaries of time and space.

Biblical Numerology

Biblical numerology uncovers the symbolic meanings and significance of numbers within the context of the Bible, revealing a rich tapestry of divine messages and spiritual truths.

1. Sacred Number Seven :

- The number 7 holds immense importance in the Bible, signifying completeness and divine perfection.

- Explore instances such as the seven days of creation and the seven seals in Revelation.

2. Forty and Trials :

- The number 40 frequently appears in the Bible, symbolizing a period of trial, testing, or preparation.

- Discuss events like the 40 days and nights of rain during Noah's Ark and Jesus' 40 days of fasting in the wilderness.

3. Number Twelve and Divine Governance :

- The number 12 is associated with governance and divine order, seen in the twelve tribes of Israel and the twelve apostles.

- Explore how this number represents completeness in God's chosen people.

4. Numerical Patterns in Prophecy :

- Prophecies in the Bible often include numerical symbolism, such as Daniel's seventy weeks.

- Discuss how understanding the numeric elements enhances the interpretation of biblical prophecies.

5. **Triune God and the Number Three :**

- The concept of the Holy Trinity embodies the number three, highlighting the Father, Son, and Holy Spirit.

- Explore how the number three signifies divine perfection and completeness.

6. **Symbolism in Names and Genealogies :**

- Names and genealogies in the Bible often carry numeric significance, revealing hidden meanings.

- Discuss examples where the numeric value of names contributes to the overall message.

Biblical numerology goes beyond mere counting; it's a lens through which believers interpret divine messages and discern deeper spiritual truths. The repetition of certain numbers in the Bible isn't coincidental but intentional, inviting readers to explore the hidden meanings encoded within the numerical fabric of sacred texts.

Vedic Numerology in Hinduism

Vedic Numerology in Hinduism unveils a rich tradition where numbers are deeply intertwined with spiritual beliefs, cosmic cycles, and the very fabric of existence.

1. Foundations in Vedic Texts :

- Explore how Vedic numerology is rooted in ancient scriptures like the Vedas and Upanishads.

- Discuss the significance of numbers in hymns, rituals, and cosmic insights.

2. Navagrahas and Nine Planets :

- The Navagrahas, or nine planets, play a vital role in Vedic numerology.

- Discuss how each planet is associated with a specific number and influences different aspects of life.

3. Astrology and Numerology Integration :

- Vedic numerology seamlessly integrates with astrology, enhancing the depth of cosmic insights.

- Explore how birthdates and names are analyzed numerologically for astrological interpretations.

4. Powerful Number Nine :

- The number 9 holds special significance in Vedic numerology, symbolizing completeness and attainment.

- Discuss its connection to auspicious rituals and spiritual accomplishments.

5. Yugas and Cosmic Cycles :

- Vedic numerology is entwined with the concept of Yugas, representing different cosmic ages.

- Explore how numbers symbolize the cyclical nature of time and the evolution of consciousness.

6. Chakras and Numerical Vibrations :

- The seven chakras in Hindu philosophy are associated with specific numbers.

- Discuss how understanding these numerical vibrations aids in spiritual balance and well-being.

Vedic Numerology in Hinduism isn't just about numbers; it's a holistic system that connects the microcosm of individual lives to the macrocosm of the universe. It invites individuals to navigate the journey of life with a profound awareness of cosmic energies, spiritual growth, and the interconnectedness of all things.

Mayan Numerical System

The Mayan Numerical System is a fascinating ancient system that played a crucial role in Mayan culture, mathematics, and astronomy. Let's explore its unique features:

1. **Base-20 System :**

   - The Mayans used a vigesimal system, based on 20 instead of the familiar base-10 system.

   - Explore how this system influenced Mayan mathematics and calendrical calculations.

2. **Mayan Glyphs and Numerals :**

   - Mayans represented numbers using a combination of dots and bars.

   - Discuss how glyphs were employed for numerical notations, emphasizing both the visual and symbolic aspects.

3. **Tun, Katun, and Baktun :**

   - Mayans had distinct units of time, including baktun (144,000 days), katun (7,200 days), and tun (360 days).

   - Explore how these units were crucial in Mayan long-count calendar calculations.

4. **Astronomical Significance :**

   - The Mayans integrated their numerical system into astronomical observations and predictions.

- Discuss how celestial events were tied to numerical cycles, such as the Venus cycle.

5. Numeric Glyphs in Art and Architecture :

- Numeric symbols appeared in Mayan art, architecture, and monuments.

- Explore examples of numerical representations in famous Mayan structures like Tikal.

6. Hieroglyphic Writing and Numbers :

- The Mayans used hieroglyphic writing for both words and numbers.

- Discuss how numerical notations were incorporated into inscriptions and stelae.

Understanding the Mayan Numerical System offers a glimpse into the sophisticated mathematical and astronomical knowledge of this ancient civilization. The vigesimal system, coupled with intricate calendrical calculations, showcases the Mayans' profound understanding of numbers and their application in decoding the mysteries of time and space.

Numerical Symbolism in Native Cultures

Numerical symbolism in Native cultures provides a window into the spiritual beliefs and interconnectedness with nature that permeate these rich traditions.

1. Harmony with the Four Directions :

- Many Native cultures hold the number four in high esteem, representing the cardinal directions (north, south, east, west) and the balance in nature.

- Explore how ceremonies and rituals often incorporate symbolic representations of these directions.

2. The Sacred Trio :

- The number three is significant in Native cultures, embodying concepts like past, present, and future or the interconnectedness of mind, body, and spirit.

- Discuss how triads manifest in stories, ceremonies, and artistic expressions.

3. Cycles of Seven :

- The number seven holds spiritual significance, representing the cycles of the moon or the seven stars of the Pleiades.

- Explore how rituals may align with lunar phases, emphasizing the interconnectedness of the natural world.

4. Numerical Representation in Art :

- Native art often incorporates numerical symbols, reflecting spiritual beliefs and the relationship between humans and the environment.

- Discuss examples of numerical motifs in traditional crafts, pottery, and paintings.

5. The Medicine Wheel :

- The Medicine Wheel, often divided into four quadrants, is a sacred symbol in many Native cultures.

- Explore how each quadrant represents different aspects of life, such as emotions, physical health, mental well-being, and spirituality.

6. Seven Generations Philosophy :

- Some Native cultures follow the principle of considering the impact of decisions on seven generations.

- Discuss how this philosophy reflects a deep connection to both ancestors and future descendants.

Numerical symbolism in Native cultures transcends mere counting, embodying a profound spiritual connection to the natural world. By understanding the significance of specific numbers, one gains insight into the holistic worldview that shapes Native beliefs, ceremonies, and daily life.

Basics of Numerology

Demystifying Numbers: A Guide to the Basics of Numerology

Numerology, the practice of interpreting the hidden meanings of numbers in your life, can be a powerful tool for self-discovery and understanding. If you're curious to peek behind the curtain of numbers and unlock their potential, this guide will equip you with the essential basics.

The Key Players: Core Numbers and Their Meanings:

• Birth Date Numbers: Your birth date (month, day, and year) holds the foundation of your numerology chart. By summing these digits, you arrive at your Life Path Number, revealing your innate potential and life purpose.

• Expression Number: Derived from your full name (birth name or current name), this number reflects your outward personality, communication style, and talents.

• Soul Urge Number: Hidden within your birth date, this number represents your inner desires, motivations, and what truly drives you on a soul level.

• Destiny Number: Combining your Life Path and Expression numbers, this number points towards your long-term goals, ambitions, and the eventual contribution you'll make to the world.

Mastering the Language: Decoding Single Digits:

Each number from 1 to 9 carries its own unique vibration and energy. Understanding these core messages is crucial for interpreting your numerology chart:

- 1: Leadership, independence, initiative.

- 2: Cooperation, balance, diplomacy.

- 3: Creativity, self-expression, optimism.

- 4: Stability, practicality, organization.

- 5: Adventure, freedom, adaptability.

- 6: Nurturing, responsibility, harmony.

- 7: Intuition, wisdom, seeking knowledge.

- 8: Power, ambition, manifestation.

- 9: Compassion, humanitarianism, artistry.

Beyond the Basics: Exploring Further Depths:

Once you grasp the core concepts, numerology offers a vast landscape to explore. You can delve deeper into:

• Master Numbers (11, 22, 33): These powerful numbers carry amplified vibrations and require careful navigation. Understanding their unique energies can illuminate your potential for greatness.

• Compatibility: Analyze numerology charts of yourself and others to uncover strengths and challenges in relationships, be it romantic, professional, or personal.

• Life Cycles: Numerology can map out significant periods in your life, shedding light on potential challenges and opportunities for growth.

Remember: Numerology isn't a deterministic blueprint or fortune-telling tool. It's a dynamic language of self-discovery, offering insights into your strengths, weaknesses, and potential paths. With an open mind and a playful spirit, you can embark on a fascinating journey through the world of numbers and unlock their hidden messages for your life.

This guide provides a basic framework for understanding numerology. As you delve deeper, countless resources await, from books and websites to practitioners who can offer personalized guidance. So, embrace the magic of numbers, explore their hidden whispers, and see where this enchanting journey takes you!

The Core Numbers: Decoding the Single Digits

In the realm of numerology, the single digits from 1 to 9 aren't just numbers on a page; they're vibrant characters with unique personalities, strengths, and challenges. Each one vibrates with its own distinct energy, influencing your thoughts, actions, and the path you navigate in life. Understanding these core numbers is like learning a new language—it unlocks a deeper understanding of your personal numerology chart and the hidden messages woven into your life.

Here's a glimpse into the essence of each core number:

1: The Independent Pioneer

- Keywords: Leadership, ambition, originality, independence, self-reliance

- Traits: Driven, confident, assertive, creative, goal-oriented

- Challenges: Arrogance, stubbornness, impatience, domineering tendencies

2: The Harmonious Mediator

- Keywords: Cooperation, diplomacy, balance, sensitivity, intuition

- Traits: Empathetic, supportive, adaptable, peace-loving, intuitive

- Challenges: Overly sensitive, indecisive, easily influenced, self-doubt

3: The Creative Communicator

- Keywords: Self-expression, optimism, joy, imagination, artistic talent

- Traits: Enthusiastic, expressive, social, imaginative, inspiring

- Challenges: Scattered energy, superficiality, self-centeredness, mood swings

4: The Stable Builder

- Keywords: Practicality, organization, discipline, reliability, hard work

- Traits: Dependable, grounded, methodical, loyal, responsible

- Challenges: Inflexibility, rigidity, workaholism, resistance to change

5: The Free-Spirited Adventurer

- Keywords: Freedom, adaptability, curiosity, versatility, sensuality

- Traits: Energetic, adventurous, resourceful, adaptable, open-minded

- Challenges: Restlessness, impulsiveness, irresponsibility, difficulty with commitment

6: The Nurturing Caregiver

- Keywords: Love, compassion, responsibility, harmony, domesticity

- Traits: Loving, supportive, nurturing, protective, community-oriented

- Challenges: Martyrdom, perfectionism, controlling tendencies, self-sacrifice

7: The Intuitive Seeker

- Keywords: Knowledge, wisdom, spirituality, analysis, introspection

- Traits: Analytical, introspective, intellectual, independent, spiritual

- Challenges: Isolation, cynicism, skepticism, overthinking, disconnection

8: The Empowered Achiever

- Keywords: Power, abundance, authority, business acumen, manifestation

- Traits: Ambitious, confident, assertive, strategic, goal-oriented

- Challenges: Workaholism, materialism, ruthlessness, obsession with control

9: The Compassionate Humanitarian

- Keywords: Universal love, humanitarianism, creativity, idealism, generosity

- Traits: Compassionate, selfless, creative, idealistic, wise

- Challenges: Escapism, impracticality, oversensitivity, difficulty with boundaries

Remember, these are just the foundational energies of each number. Their expressions can be nuanced and multifaceted, depending on their placement within your numerology chart and the unique blend of numbers that make up your personal profile. As you delve deeper into numerology, you'll discover how these core numbers interact and influence different aspects of your life, offering valuable insights into your personality, relationships, career, and soul's journey.

The Birth Number: A Seed of Potential

In the vibrant language of numerology, your birth date holds a special significance. It's not just a marker in time; it's a numerical tapestry woven with threads of purpose, potential, and unique vibrations. Within this date lies your birth number, the seed from which your entire numerological profile blossoms.

Think of your birth date (month, day, and year) as a magical recipe. Each digit contributes its own distinct essence – the adventurous spirit of a "5," the nurturing warmth of a "6," the analytical precision of an "8." By adding these digits together (excluding leading zeros), you arrive at your birth number, a single-digit expression of your core potential and life theme.

The journey to unveiling your birth number is simple yet profound. Let's imagine your birth date is November 15, 1978. We simply sum all the digits: 11 + 15 + 1978 = 1994. Then, we reduce this number to a single digit by adding them again: 1 + 9 + 9 + 4 = 23. This, your birth number, holds the key to understanding your inherent strengths, challenges, and the unique path you're meant to walk.

The birth number isn't a rigid destiny; it's a luminous compass guiding you towards your true north. It reveals your core essence – are you a natural leader like a "1," a creative spark like a "3," or a thoughtful strategist like a "7"? By understanding your birth number, you gain insights into your motivations, talents, and the areas where you can truly blossom.

But the journey doesn't end there. Your birth number forms the foundation of your numerological chart, a rich tapestry woven with other influential numbers like your Expression Number (based on your full name), Soul Urge Number (hidden within your birth date), and Destiny Number (a combination of your Life Path and Expression). Each adds another layer, revealing different facets of your personality, desires, and long-term goals.

So, embark on this exciting exploration of your birth number. It's a gateway to understanding yourself on a deeper level, embracing your potential, and navigating the unique path that awaits you. Remember, the world of numerology is a treasure trove waiting to be discovered, and your birth number is the key that unlocks its hidden doors.

Building the Numerology Toolbox

R eady to roll up your sleeves and start exploring the hidden messages in your numbers? Just like any skilled craftsperson, a numerologist needs the right tools to uncover the numerical symphony that makes up your life. This chapter will equip you with the essential instruments to begin crafting your personal numerology chart and unlock the wisdom it holds.

Essential Tools for Charting Your Number Journey:

1. Numerology Calculator: While you can certainly perform the calculations by hand, a numerology calculator can streamline the process and ensure accuracy. Numerous online calculators are available for free, or you can opt for numerology apps for convenient access on your phone or tablet.
2. Pen and Paper (or a Digital Notebook): Whether you prefer the tactile feel of a physical notebook or the convenience of digital notes, a place to record your calculations, interpretations, and reflections is essential. This becomes your personal numerology journal, where you'll track your journey and uncover patterns over time.
3. Chart Templates: Visualizing your numerology chart can enhance understanding and reveal connections between different numbers. Download or create templates that outline the various positions in a numerology chart, allowing you to fill in your numbers as you calculate them.
4. Numerology Resources: Surround yourself with reliable books, websites, or online courses that provide in-depth information about numerology, number meanings, and interpretation techniques. Seek reputable sources that offer balanced perspectives and align with your learning style.

Now, let's assemble the key components of your numerology toolbox:

1. Birth Date Numbers: These numbers, derived from your birth date,

form the foundation of your chart. They reveal your Life Path Number, Soul Urge Number, and other significant insights.

2. Name Numbers: Your full name (birth name or current name) holds numerical vibrations that express your personality, talents, and communication style. These numbers reveal your Expression Number, Heart's Desire Number, Personality Number, and more.

3. Master Numbers: These special numbers (11, 22, 33) hold intensified energy and require careful interpretation. They signal a heightened potential for growth and transformation.

With these tools in hand, you're ready to dive into the calculations and start painting your unique numerological portrait. Remember, numerology is an ongoing exploration, not a one-time reading. As you deepen your understanding and uncover new layers of meaning, your toolbox will continue to expand, revealing the hidden wisdom of numbers that guides your journey of self-discovery.

Unveiling the Enigma: Understanding Master Numbers

In the vibrant tapestry of numerology, certain digits stand out not just for their unique energy, but also for their amplified power. These are the Master Numbers, rare and potent vibrations that hold immense potential but also require careful navigation. Unlike the single digits (1-9), Master Numbers (11, 22, 33) pulsate with a higher frequency, demanding a deeper understanding and a conscious approach to unlock their true essence.

Master Number 11: The Visionary Idealist

This number embodies the visionary, the pioneer, the dreamer who sees beyond the limitations of the ordinary. It carries the energy of innovation, inspiration, and the relentless pursuit of a higher purpose. However, the 11 can also struggle with idealism, perfectionism, and sensitivity, often navigating the world feeling misunderstood or alone.

Master Number 22: The Master Builder

The 22 vibrates with the power of creation, leadership, and manifestation on a grand scale. It embodies the architect, the builder, the one who brings ambitious visions to life. Yet, the 22 can also face challenges with practicality, balancing ambition with compassion, and overcoming the fear of failure.

Master Number 33: The Master Teacher

This number carries the energy of universal love, compassion, and the desire to serve humanity. It embodies the teacher, the healer, the one who guides others towards their highest potential. However, the 33 can also struggle with overwhelm, taking on the burdens of others, and finding balance between giving and self-care.

Understanding Master Numbers:

• Not everyone has a Master Number. Their presence in your numerology chart requires careful analysis, as they can significantly influence your life path and purpose.

• Master Numbers don't replace single digits. They exist on a higher level, adding an extra layer of complexity and potential to your core number vibrations.

• Master Numbers require conscious integration. Their immense energy can be overwhelming if not channeled constructively. Developing self-awareness, patience, and a strong sense of purpose is crucial for harnessing their true power.

Exploring Master Numbers in your chart:

If you have a Master Number as your Life Path or Soul Urge Number, it indicates a powerful calling and a unique responsibility to contribute to the world.

• Master Numbers in other positions of your chart can add specific strengths and challenges to those areas.

Remember, Master Numbers are not shortcuts to success or guarantees of greatness. They are invitations to embrace a higher level of awareness, responsibility, and service. By understanding their potential and challenges, you can navigate their energy with grace and wisdom, unlocking the transformative power they hold within.

Delving into the world of Master Numbers is a journey of self-discovery, a chance to connect with your innate potential and embrace the challenges and opportunities that come with wielding such powerful vibrations. So, if you have a Master Number in your chart, consider it a special gift, a call to rise above the ordinary and illuminate the world with your unique light.

Unlocking Your Personal Numerology - Charting Your Unique Journey

With your numerology toolbox assembled and Master Numbers deciphered, it's time to embark on the most exciting part of your numerological journey – creating your personal chart and unlocking its hidden messages. This is where theory meets practice, where the abstract language of numbers transforms into a personalized roadmap for self-discovery and growth.

Step 1: Laying the Foundation – Birth Date Numbers

It all begins with your birth date. This seemingly unassuming sequence of numbers holds the key to your Life Path Number, the core essence of your life journey and purpose. Add the digits of your month, day, and year together (excluding leading zeros) and reduce the sum to a single digit (between 1 and 9) if needed. This is your Life Path Number – the guiding light illuminating your inherent strengths, challenges, and the path you're meant to walk.

Step 2: Unveiling Your Inner Voice – Name Numbers

Your full name isn't just a label; it's a potent vibration reflecting your outward personality and communication style. Each letter holds a corresponding number, and by using a numerology chart you can decode your Expression Number, Heart's Desire Number, Personality Number, and more. These numbers reveal your talents, desires, how you project yourself to the world, and even hidden aspects of your inner self.

Step 3: Connecting the Dots – Chart Positions and Interpretations

Now, it's time to piece together your personal numerology chart. Think of it as a constellation, where each number occupies a specific position and influences others. Different numerology schools use slightly varying chart layouts, but here are some key positions:

• Life Path Number: Your core essence and journey.

• Soul Urge Number: Your inner desires and motivations.

• Destiny Number: Your long-term goals and ultimate contribution.

• Expression Number: Your outward personality and communication style.

• Challenges Numbers: Areas where you need to work on and grow.

• Karmic Debt Numbers: Lessons from past lives you're meant to learn.

Interpreting these numbers requires research and introspection. Refer to reliable numerology books, websites, or even consult a professional numerologist for guidance. Remember, understanding the nuances of different number combinations and their interactions is key to accurately uncovering your personal story.

Step 4: Embracing the Journey – Growth and Transformation

Numerology isn't a static snapshot; it's a dynamic conversation between you and the numbers that influence your life. As you learn more about your core vibrations, challenges, and potential, you can use this knowledge to:

• Make informed decisions: Career choices, relationships, personal goals – numerology can offer insights to guide you towards alignment with your true purpose.

• Embrace your strengths: Understanding your inherent talents and skills can boost your confidence and empower you to flourish in areas where you excel.

• Work on your challenges: Numerology can highlight areas where you need to grow, providing valuable pointers for personal development and overcoming obstacles.

• Connect with your soul's purpose: Uncovering your Life Path and Soul Urge Numbers can give you a deeper sense of meaning and direction, guiding you towards your unique contributions to the world.

Remember, your numerology chart is a living document, evolving as you navigate life's experiences. Keep exploring, experimenting, and learning. As you deepen your understanding and integrate its wisdom into your choices, you'll unlock the transformative power of numbers and chart a course towards a life filled with self-discovery, purpose, and fulfillment.

Your Numerical Tapestry: Calculating Your Numerology Blueprint

Numerology, the enchanting practice of interpreting the hidden meanings within numbers, offers a unique lens through which to understand yourself and your life's journey. Ready to embark on this fascinating exploration? Let's dive into the exciting world of calculating your own numerological blueprint!

Step 1: Laying the Foundation with Birth Date Numbers

Your birthdate, a seemingly ordinary sequence, holds the key to your Life Path Number, the core essence of your life's purpose and potential. To unlock it, simply add the digits of your month, day, and year (excluding leading zeros) and reduce the sum to a single digit (between 1 and 9) if needed. This number, your Life Path, illuminates the inherent strengths, challenges, and the path you're meant to walk.

Step 2: Unveiling Your Inner Voice through Name Numbers

Your full name, more than just a label, is a vibrant vibration reflecting your outward personality and communication style. Each letter corresponds to a specific number, and by using a numerology chart, you can decode your Expression Number, revealing how you project yourself to the world. Explore further to discover your Heart's Desire Number, unveiling your inner yearnings, and your Personality Number, showcasing the hidden facets of your self-image.

Step 3: Building Your Numerology Chart: A Constellation of Numbers

Think of your personal numerology chart as a constellation, where each number occupies a specific position and influences others. Different schools use slightly varying layouts, but some key positions include:

• Life Path Number: Your core essence and life journey.

• Soul Urge Number: Your inner desires and motivations.

• Destiny Number: Your long-term goals and ultimate contribution.

• Expression Number: Your outward personality and communication style.

• Challenges Numbers: Areas where you need to work on and grow.

• Karmic Debt Numbers: Lessons from past lives you're meant to learn.

Decoding these numbers requires research and introspection. Reliable numerology books, websites, or even consulting a professional numerologist can offer valuable guidance. Remember, understanding the nuances of different number combinations and their interactions is key to accurately uncovering your personal story.

Step 4: Embracing the Journey: Growth and Transformation with Numbers as Your Guide

Numerology isn't a static snapshot; it's a dynamic conversation between you and the numbers that influence your life. As you learn more about your core vibrations, challenges, and potential, you can use this knowledge to:

• Make informed choices: Career paths, relationships, personal goals – numerology can offer insights to guide you towards alignment with your true purpose.

• Embrace your strengths: Understanding your inherent talents and skills can boost your confidence and empower you to flourish in areas where you excel.

• Work on your challenges: Numerology can highlight areas where you need to grow, providing valuable pointers for personal development and overcoming obstacles.

• Connect with your soul's purpose: Uncovering your Life Path and Soul Urge Numbers can give you a deeper sense of meaning and direction, guiding you towards your unique contributions to the world.

Remember, your numerology chart is a living document, evolving as you navigate life's experiences. Keep exploring, experimenting, and learning. As you deepen your understanding and integrate its wisdom into your choices, you'll unlock the transformative power of numbers and chart a course towards a life filled with self-discovery, purpose, and fulfillment.

This is just the beginning of your personal numerological adventure! Feel free to explore further and ask any questions about specific chart interpretations, number interactions, or your unique numerological tapestry. The journey of self-discovery awaits, guided by the vibrant whispers of your personal numbers.

How to calculate the life path number?

———

S ample 1 and 2

Discovering your Life Path Number is an exciting journey into the world of numerology. It's a simple process that involves adding up specific components of your birthdate to unveil a number that holds unique significance for your life.

Here's a step-by-step guide :

1. **Write Down Your Birthdate:**

   • Start with your complete birthdate, including the day, month, and year.

2. **Convert to Numerals:**

   • Convert each component of your birthdate into a single-digit number. For example, if you were born on May 10, 1990, you'd convert it to 5 (month), 1 (day), and $1+9+9+0 = 19$, then further reduce 19 to $1+9 = 10$, and finally reduce 10 to $1+0 = 1$ (year).

3. **Add the Numbers:**

   • Add the single-digit numbers from each component together. Using the example above, you'd add 5 (month) + 1 (day) + 1 (year) = 7.

4. **Life Path Number:**

   • The final sum is your Life Path Number. In this example, if the total is 7, then your Life Path Number is 7.

5. **Explore the Meaning:**

• Each Life Path Number has unique characteristics and traits associated with it. Take some time to explore the significance of your Life Path Number and what it reveals about your personality and life journey.

Remember, this process is not about predicting the future but gaining insights into your strengths, challenges, and potential paths in life. It's a tool for self-discovery that many find both insightful and empowering.

Sample 2

Calculating your Life Path Number is a simple yet powerful step in your numerology journey! Here's how you can do it:

1. Gather your birth date: You'll need the month, day, and year of your birth. Let's use July 15, 1989 as an example.

2. Add the digits of your birth date:

• Month: July = 7

• Day: 15 = 1 + 5

• Year: 1989 = 1 + 9 + 8 + 9 = 27

3. Reduce the sum to a single digit (between 1 and 9):

• Add the single-digit numbers you got in step 2: 7 + 6 + 27 = 40

• If the sum is still two digits, add those digits further: 4 + 0 = 4

Therefore, your Life Path Number in this example is 4!

Here are some things to keep in mind:

• Ignore leading zeros in your birth year.

• Master Numbers (11, 22, and 33) are treated as single digits if you reach them during the reduction process.

Once you have your Life Path Number, you can start exploring its meaning and how it influences various aspects of your life. Remember, numerology is a journey, not a destination. Keep learning, experimenting, and discovering the hidden messages within your personal numbers!

Calculating your Life Path Number involves breaking down your birthdate into single digits and summing them up. Let's break down the process in a simple and clear way :

1. **Write Down Your Birthdate:**

   • Start with your full birthdate, including the day, month, and year.

2. **Convert Each Component:**

   • Convert each part of your birthdate into a single-digit number. For example, if your birthdate is May 15, 1985:

   • Month (May): 5

   • Day: $1 + 5 = 6$

   • Year: $1 + 9 + 8 + 5 = 23$, then further reduce 23 to $2 + 3 = 5$.

3. **Add the Single-Digit Numbers:**

   • Add the single-digit numbers obtained from the month, day, and year. Using the example above: 5 (month) + 6 (day) + 5 (year) = 16.

4. **Reduce to a Single Digit:**

   • If the sum is a two-digit number, further reduce it to a single digit by adding the individual digits. In this example, $1 + 6 = 7$.

5. **Life Path Number:**

   • The final single-digit sum is your Life Path Number. In this example, the Life Path Number is 7.

Understanding your Life Path Number can offer insights into your personality, strengths, and potential life path. It's a fascinating aspect of numerology that many find enlightening and enjoyable to explore.

Each Life Path Number from 1 to 9 carries its own unique set of characteristics and influences various aspects of your life, including personality, strengths, challenges, and potential paths. Let's delve into the essence of each Life Path:

Life Path 1:

• Keywords: Leadership, independence, initiative, originality, ambition

• Strengths: Confident, assertive, self-reliant, creative, goal-oriented

• Challenges: Stubbornness, impatience, arrogance, tendency to dominate

• Life Path: Individuals on this path are natural leaders, born to pioneer and innovate. They thrive on independence and setting their own course, often excelling in entrepreneurial ventures, management roles, or artistic pursuits.

Life Path 2:

• Keywords: Cooperation, diplomacy, balance, sensitivity, intuition

• Strengths: Empathetic, supportive, adaptable, peaceful, intuitive

• Challenges: Indecisiveness, oversensitivity, codependency, difficulty with conflict

• Life Path: Individuals on this path are natural diplomats and peacemakers. They excel at building relationships, mediating conflicts, and fostering harmony. Their strengths shine in professions like social work, therapy, teaching, and diplomacy.

Life Path 3:

• Keywords: Self-expression, optimism, joy, creativity, artistic talent

• Strengths: Enthusiastic, expressive, imaginative, adaptable, communicative

• Challenges: Scattered energy, superficiality, self-centeredness, mood swings

• Life Path: Individuals on this path are natural communicators and performers. They bring joy and creativity to everything they do, excelling in artistic fields, entertainment, sales, and communication.

Life Path 4:

• Keywords: Practicality, organization, discipline, reliability, hard work

• Strengths: Dependable, grounded, methodical, loyal, responsible

• Challenges: Inflexibility, rigidity, workaholism, resistance to change

• Life Path: Individuals on this path are the builders and organizers. They have a strong work ethic and find satisfaction in creating structure and stability. They excel in careers like engineering, finance, management, and construction.

Life Path 5:

• Keywords: Freedom, adaptability, curiosity, versatility, sensuality

• Strengths: Energetic, adventurous, resourceful, adaptable, open-minded

• Challenges: Restlessness, impulsiveness, irresponsibility, difficulty with commitment

• Life Path: Individuals on this path are free spirits who crave adventure and new experiences. They excel in diverse fields like travel, marketing, sales, and creative endeavors.

Life Path 6:

• Keywords: Love, compassion, responsibility, harmony, domesticity

• Strengths: Loving, supportive, nurturing, protective, community-oriented

• Challenges: Martyr tendencies, perfectionism, controlling behavior, self-sacrifice

• Life Path: Individuals on this path are natural caregivers and nurturers. They excel in professions like healthcare, teaching, social work, and family-oriented careers.

Life Path 7:

• Keywords: Knowledge, wisdom, spirituality, analysis, introspection

• Strengths: Analytical, introspective, intellectual, independent, spiritual

• Challenges: Isolation, cynicism, skepticism, overthinking, disconnection

• Life Path: Individuals on this path are natural seekers of truth and knowledge. They excel in research, academia, philosophy, and introspective fields.

Life Path 8:

• Keywords: Power, abundance, authority, business acumen, manifestation

• Strengths: Ambitious, confident, assertive, strategic, goal-oriented

• Challenges: Workaholism, materialism, ruthlessness, obsession with control

• Life Path: Individuals on this path are natural leaders and power players. They excel in business, finance, politics, and any field where ambition and strategy are key.

Life Path 9:

• Keywords: Universal love, humanitarianism, creativity, idealism, generosity

• Strengths: Compassionate, selfless, creative, idealistic, wise

• Challenges: Escapism, impracticality, oversensitivity, difficulty with boundaries

• Life Path: Individuals on this path are natural humanitarians and idealists. They excel in creative fields, social work, environmentalism, and anything that allows them to contribute to the greater good.

Remember, these are just core descriptions, and your individual expression of your Life Path Number will be unique and nuanced. Consider the influences of other numbers in your numerology chart, your life experiences, and your own personal journey to gain a deeper understanding of your true potential and purpose.

Unveiling Your Expression Number

Unveiling your Expression Number is another exciting aspect of numerology that reveals insights into your natural talents and how you express yourself in the world. Here's a simple guide to calculating and understanding your Expression Number :

1. **Write Down Your Full Birth Name:**

   • Use the name given to you at birth, including your first, middle, and last names.

2. **Assign Numerical Values:**

   • Assign each letter of the alphabet a numerical value based on its position (A=1, B=2, C=3, and so on).

   • Write down the numerical values for each letter in your full birth name.

3. **Add the Numbers:**

   • Add the numerical values for all the letters in your name.

4. **Reduce to a Single Digit:**

   • If the sum is a two-digit number, reduce it to a single digit by adding the individual digits.

5. **Expression Number:**

   • The final single-digit sum is your Expression Number. This number reflects your natural talents, strengths, and how you express yourself in the world.

Now, let's briefly explore the potential meanings of each Expression Number

Ah, the Expression Number! This vibrant gem in your numerology chart shines a light on how you project yourself to the world and express your inner voice. It's like your personal communication style, the way you interact, and the impression you leave on others. So, how do you unlock this fascinating aspect of your numerology blueprint?

Unveiling the Code:

To find your Expression Number, you'll need your full birth name (the one used most consistently in your life). Buckle up, it's number time!

1. Assign a numerical value to each letter in your name. Refer to a numerology chart, where A = 1, B = 2, and so on. For example, if your name is "Sarah Jones," your numerical code would be 19 1 18 8 15 5.
2. Add up all the numbers. In this case, 19 + 1 + 18 + 8 + 15 + 5 = 66.
3. Reduce the sum to a single digit (between 1 and 9). If the sum is a two-digit number, add those digits further. For example, 66 = 6 + 6 = 12. So, in this case, Sarah's Expression Number is 12.

Interpreting the Expression:

Now, the fun begins! Each single-digit Expression Number carries its own unique energy and tendencies:

• 1: The Leader/Pioneer: Confident, outgoing, independent, assertive, innovative.

• 2: The Diplomat/Harmonizer: Sensitive, cooperative, adaptable, supportive, peace-loving.

• 3: The Creative/Communicator: Enthusiastic, expressive, imaginative, joyful, social.

• 4: The Builder/Organizer: Practical, reliable, disciplined, grounded, detail-oriented.

- 5: The Adventurer/Free Spirit: Adaptable, curious, resourceful, versatile, impulsive.

- 6: The Nurturer/Caregiver: Loving, responsible, protective, compassionate, harmonious.

- 7: The Seeker/Analyst: Introspective, intellectual, analytical, spiritual, independent.

- 8: The Achiever/Power Player: Ambitious, confident, strategic, authoritative, goal-oriented.

- 9: The Humanitarian/Idealist: Compassionate, selfless, creative, idealistic, wise.

Remember, your Expression Number is just one piece of your complex numerological puzzle. Consider it a key ingredient in the recipe of your personality, blending with other influences in your chart to create your unique flavor.

Beyond the Surface:

Your Expression Number isn't just about how you come across initially. It also reveals:

- Communication style: Are you a direct communicator like a "1" or a subtler persuader like a "5"?

- Strengths and challenges: Knowing your dominant energy can help you leverage your strengths and navigate your challenges in communication and self-expression.

- Potential career paths: Your Expression Number can offer insights into jobs where your natural communication style would thrive.

Remember, the journey of self-discovery through numerology is ongoing. As you explore your Expression Number and integrate its wisdom, you'll unlock a deeper understanding of who you are and how you best express your unique essence to the world.

Discovering your Soul Urge Number

Delves into the innermost desires and motivations that drive your true self. Let's explore a simple guide to calculating and understanding your Soul Urge Number :

1. **Write Down Your Full Birth Name:**

   • Use the name given to you at birth, including your first, middle, and last names.

2. **Assign Numerical Values:**

   • Assign each letter of the alphabet a numerical value based on its position (A=1, B=2, C=3, and so on).

   • Write down the numerical values for each vowel in your full birth name (A, E, I, O, U).

3. **Add the Numbers:**

   • Add the numerical values for all the vowels in your name.

4. **Reduce to a Single Digit:**

   • If the sum is a two-digit number, reduce it to a single digit by adding the individual digits.

5. **Soul Urge Number:**

   • The final single-digit sum is your Soul Urge Number. This number reflects your innermost desires, motivations, and the essence of your being.

Now, let's briefly explore the potential meanings of each Soul Urge Number :

The Soul Urge Number, nestled within your numerology chart, whispers the secret desires of your heart. It reveals the passions, motivations, and deepest yearnings that drive you from within, shaping your choices and propelling you towards your soul's true fulfillment. So, are you ready to embark on this introspective journey and uncover your hidden desires?

Unveiling the Whisper:

To discover your Soul Urge Number, you'll need your trusty vowels! Unlike the Expression Number, which focuses on outward expression, the Soul Urge dives into the inner world. Here's how to unlock its secrets:

1. Gather your vowels: Write down your full birth name (the one used most consistently in your life). Now, focus on the vowels, like the "a" in Sarah or the "u" in John. Ignore consonants and punctuation.
2. Assign a numerical value to each vowel: A = 1, E = 5, I = 9, O = 6, and U = 3. For example, in "Sarah Jones," your vowel code would be 1 5 18 9.
3. Add up all the vowel numbers. In this case, 1 + 5 + 18 + 9 = 33.
4. Reduce the sum to a single digit (between 1 and 9). If the sum is a two-digit number, add those digits further. Master Numbers (11, 22, and 33) are treated as single digits unless reduced further and reaching another Master Number. So, for "Sarah Jones," the Soul Urge Number would be 33, a Master Number representing profound creativity, idealism, and service to humanity.

Interpreting the Yearning:

Now, you can delve into the unique energy of your Soul Urge Number:

• 1: The Pioneer Soul: Craves independence, leadership, and innovation. Seeks to break free and forge their own path.

• 2: The Harmonious Soul: Desires balance, cooperation, and peace. Yearns for deep connections and harmonious relationships.

- 3: The Creative Soul: Driven by self-expression, joy, and imagination. Seeks to bring beauty and light to the world through their talents.

- 4: The Stable Soul: Desire predictability, order, and structure. Finds their purpose in building something solid and sustainable.

- 5: The Adventurous Soul: Craves freedom, change, and new experiences. Yearns for exploration and a life full of variety.

- 6: The Nurturing Soul: Driven by love, compassion, and a desire to care for others. Seeks to create a safe and harmonious environment.

- 7: The Seeker Soul: Yearns for knowledge, wisdom, and spiritual understanding. Craves solitude and introspection to uncover hidden truths.

- 8: The Achiever Soul: Motivated by power, ambition, and material success. Driven to build something impactful and leave a lasting legacy.

- 9: The Humanitarian Soul: Seeks to serve humanity, promote universal love, and alleviate suffering. Driven by a sense of purpose beyond themselves.

- Master Numbers 11, 22, and 33: These numbers carry amplified energy and potential, requiring conscious channeling towards making a significant impact on the world.

Remember, your Soul Urge Number is a hidden thread woven into the tapestry of your being. It's not always readily apparent, and embracing your deepest desires may require courage and self-acceptance. However, as you honor these yearnings and integrate them into your life choices, you'll find yourself closer to living a life aligned with your soul's true purpose.

Each of the numerology numbers—Life Path, Expression, and Soul Urge—holds unique influence on personality traits and life choices. Let's explore how they shape individuals :

1. **Life Path Number Influence:**

- *Personality Traits:* The Life Path Number provides insight into one's basic nature and overarching life purpose. For example, a Life Path 1 individual may be independent and ambitious, inclined towards leadership roles.

- *Life Choices:* It can influence career choices, relationships, and major life decisions. Someone with a Life Path 5, valuing freedom, might choose diverse and adventurous career paths.

2. **Expression Number Influence:**

- *Personality Traits:* The Expression Number reveals innate talents and how one expresses themselves. An Expression 3 person may be naturally creative and communicative.

- *Life Choices:* It can guide individuals toward careers aligned with their talents. For instance, an Expression 8 person might excel in business and financial endeavors.

3. **Soul Urge Number Influence:**

- *Personality Traits:* The Soul Urge Number reflects innermost desires and motivations. Someone with a Soul Urge 6 may be nurturing and deeply connected to family.

- *Life Choices:* It shapes personal relationships, lifestyle choices, and the pursuit of passions. A Soul Urge 9 person might be drawn to humanitarian causes and a life dedicated to helping others.

Understanding these numbers can help individuals make choices aligned with their true selves. For instance, someone with a Life Path 2 might thrive in collaborative environments, influencing career and relationship choices. The Expression and Soul Urge Numbers provide additional layers, guiding individuals toward areas where they can naturally shine and find fulfillment.

It's essential to note that while numerology offers valuable insights, personal agency and external factors also play significant roles in shaping personality and life choices. Numerology serves as a tool for self-discovery, empowering individuals to make informed decisions in harmony with their inherent traits and desires.

The Intertwined Dance of Numbers:

How Life Path, Expression, and Soul Urge Shape You

In the mystical realm of numerology, three potent numbers dance together, weaving their threads into the tapestry of your personality and guiding your life choices. These are your Life Path Number, Expression Number, and Soul Urge Number, each holding a unique key to understanding who you are and where you're headed.

Life Path Number: The Core Essence

Think of your Life Path Number as the sun at the center of your numerological solar system. It represents your core essence, your inherent strengths and challenges, and the overarching journey you're meant to navigate in this life. Its influence is pervasive, shaping your motivations, goals, and the kinds of experiences you naturally gravitate towards.

For example, someone with a Life Path Number 3 might possess inherent creativity and a desire to bring joy to others. This might manifest in careers like acting, music, or teaching, where they can express themselves and bring light to the world.

Expression Number: The Public Persona

Your Expression Number acts like a window to your soul, the face you present to the world. It reveals your communication style, how you interact with others, and the first impression you leave. This number influences how you project your strengths and vulnerabilities, shaping how you navigate relationships, assert yourself, and communicate your ideas.

A person with an Expression Number 8, for example, might naturally exude confidence and authority. They might excel in leadership roles or persuasive careers, where their strong presence and strategic communication skills shine.

Soul Urge Number: The Hidden Compass

Deep within your being lies your Soul Urge Number, a silent whisper of your heart's desires. This number reveals your deepest yearnings, the passions that motivate you from within, and the kind of life that truly satisfies your soul. It might not always be immediately obvious or aligned with your current circumstances, but its pull can be powerful, guiding you towards choices that bring you closer to your true fulfillment.

Someone with a Soul Urge Number 2, for example, might crave harmony and deep connections. This might lead them towards careers in counseling, mediation, or building strong communities, where their desire for balance and peace can flourish.

The Interplay: A Symphony of Numbers

It's important to understand that these numbers aren't isolated entities. They interact and influence each other, creating a unique symphony that defines your personality and life journey. Your Life Path might set the overall theme, your Expression Number the instrument you play, and your Soul Urge the melody that guides your song.

For instance, someone with a Life Path 5 as a free spirit might find their expressive outlet through a career in travel writing (Expression Number 3) that fulfills their thirst for adventure and new experiences (Soul Urge 5).

Making Choice with Awareness:

As you become more aware of these three influential numbers, you can use their guidance to make more conscious choices in your life. Your Life Path can act as a compass, pointing you towards opportunities that align with your purpose. Your Expression Number can help you refine your communication and navigate relationships more effectively. And your Soul Urge can nudge you towards experiences that spark your inner fire and lead you closer to true fulfillment.

Remember, numerology isn't about determinism; it's about empowerment. By understanding the energies that influence you, you can make choices that resonate with your authentic self and create a life that feels rich, meaningful, and aligned with your unique song.

So, explore your numbers, delve into their depths, and let them guide you on your own personal dance of self-discovery. It's a journey filled with wonder, potential, and the ever-unfolding story of who you truly are.

Numerology and Relationships: Unlocking Compatibility and Harmony

Relationships, a cornerstone of human life, can be beautiful, tumultuous, and everything in between. Numerology, the study of the mystical relationships between numbers and life, offers a unique perspective on navigating these intricate bonds. While it shouldn't dictate your choices, it can provide valuable insights into compatibility, strengths, and potential challenges in your relationships.

Life Path Numbers: The Core Essence Match

The foundation of numerological relationship analysis lies in your Life Path Numbers. These core essence numbers reveal your innate strengths, challenges, and life purposes. Matching Life Path Numbers can offer clues about the potential synergies and clashes between two individuals.

• Complementary Numbers: Some Life Path Numbers naturally complement each other, creating a harmonious balance. For example, a grounded and practical Life Path 4 might find stability and support in a creative and expressive Life Path 3.

• Challenging Numbers: Other Life Paths may present more challenges, but also opportunities for growth. A fiercely independent Life Path 1 might clash with a nurturing and cooperative Life Path 6, but if they learn to respect and value each other's differences, they can create a dynamic and mutually beneficial relationship.

Beyond Life Paths: A Constellation of Numbers

Life Path Numbers offer a starting point, but a comprehensive relationship analysis dives deeper. Your Expression Numbers showcase how you communicate and project yourself, influencing how you interact with your partner. Soul Urge Numbers reveal your hidden desires and deepest aspirations, impacting your long-term compatibility and shared goals.

Challenges and Growth:

Numerology also highlights potential areas of friction in relationships. Certain number combinations might indicate tendencies towards communication issues, power struggles, or differing emotional needs. Recognizing these challenges through numerology can allow you to work on them proactively, fostering understanding and building stronger bonds.

Remember:

• Numerology is not a definitive recipe for relationship success. Individual choices, experiences, and personal growth play a crucial role.

• Use numerology as a tool for self-awareness and understanding your partner, not as a means to judge or predict the future.

• Focus on the strengths and potential synergies revealed by your numbers, and use the challenges as opportunities for growth and communication.

Ultimately, the success of your relationships depends on mutual effort, respect, and understanding. Numerology can act as a guiding light, helping you navigate the complexities of love and connection with greater awareness and insight.

As you explore the fascinating world of numerology and its impact on relationships, remember to keep an open mind, embrace communication, and prioritize the love and connection that fuels every true partnership.

Numerology can offer intriguing insights into relationships by examining the compatibility of individuals based on their numerological profiles. Let's explore how numerology can play a role in understanding relationships :

1. **Life Path Compatibility:**

• Individuals with compatible Life Path Numbers often share similar fundamental traits, making it easier to understand and support each other's life journeys.

• For example, Life Path 1 and 5 individuals, both valuing independence, might appreciate and encourage each other's pursuit of personal goals.

2. Expression Number Dynamics:

• Compatibility in Expression Numbers can highlight shared interests and communication styles.

• Expression 3 individuals may find harmony with others who appreciate creativity and joyful expression, enhancing compatibility in relationships.

3. Soul Urge Harmony:

• Understanding Soul Urge Numbers can unveil shared desires and motivations, fostering emotional connection and support.

• Soul Urge 6 individuals, driven by a desire for love and family, may find deep compatibility with partners who share similar values.

4. Numerological Challenges:

• Numerology can also reveal potential challenges in relationships, especially when certain numbers clash in terms of their inherent traits and desires.

• Identifying and understanding these challenges can help partners navigate differences and work towards mutual understanding.

5. Life Choices Alignment:

- Numerology can guide couples in making decisions that align with their combined energies. It helps in choosing a compatible lifestyle, career paths, and shared goals.

- For instance, a couple with complementary Expression Numbers may find fulfillment in pursuing common creative endeavors.

6. **Personal Growth Insights:**

- Numerology not only aids in understanding compatibility but also offers insights into individual and joint personal growth.

- Couples can use numerology as a tool for self-awareness and mutual support on their journeys towards self-improvement.

It's important to note that while numerology provides interesting perspectives on compatibility, relationships are complex and multifaceted. Personalities, communication styles, and values are influenced by various factors beyond numerology. Numerology can be a fun and insightful tool for couples to explore, offering a unique lens through which to understand and strengthen their connections.

Numerology and Relationship Harmony

Within the realm of numerology, compatibility isn't about finding a perfect match, but rather about understanding the unique energies that two individuals bring to the partnership. By exploring the interplay of Life Path Numbers, Expression Numbers, and Soul Urge Numbers, we can uncover potential areas of harmony, growth, and even challenges that can help couples navigate their relationships with greater awareness and understanding.

Life Path Number Compatibility:

● 1 and 5: Both crave independence and adventure, sparking excitement and shared passions.

● 2 and 6: Their shared desire for harmony and nurturing creates a supportive and loving bond.

● 3 and 7: Intellectual stimulation and deep conversations fuel their connection.

● 4 and 8: A practical and grounded approach to life builds stability and mutual respect.

● 9 and 1: Their shared idealism and humanitarian spirit create a powerful force for positive change.

Challenges and Opportunities for Growth:

● 1 and 8: Power struggles can arise, but learning to share control and celebrate each other's strengths leads to success.

● 2 and 4: The 4's practicality might clash with the 2's emotional sensitivity, requiring open communication and understanding.

● 3 and 6: The 3's desire for freedom might conflict with the 6's need for security, but finding a balance between adventure and stability strengthens their bond.

Beyond Life Path Numbers:

● Expression Number Compatibility: Reveals how you communicate and interact, influencing how you express affection, resolve conflicts, and share ideas.

• Soul Urge Number Compatibility: Aligning your deepest desires and aspirations is crucial for long-term harmony and shared goals.

Remember:

• Numerology offers insights, not absolutes. Individual choices, communication, and commitment are paramount.

• Embrace challenges as opportunities for growth and understanding.

• Focus on the strengths and synergies revealed by your numbers, and work together to address potential differences.

• Use numerology as a tool for self-awareness and understanding, not judgment or prediction.

Prioritizing Love and Connection:

Ultimately, numerology can illuminate the path towards greater understanding and harmony in relationships. By embracing its insights, couples can navigate challenges, celebrate their unique connections, and build partnerships that thrive on mutual respect, love, and shared growth.

1. Life Path Compatibility:

- **Compatible Numbers:** Individuals with Life Path Numbers that share similar traits often have a natural understanding and compatibility. For instance, Life Path 1 might align well with 5 due to their shared independence.

- **Challenges:** Some Life Path Numbers may clash, emphasizing the importance of understanding and addressing potential differences. For example, Life Path 1 and 8 may face challenges due to their strong-willed nature.

2. Expression Number Harmony:

- **Similar Interests:** Compatibility in Expression Numbers suggests shared interests and communication styles. Expression 3 individuals, for example, might find compatibility with others who appreciate creativity and self-expression.

- **Differences:** Understanding differences in Expression Numbers can help navigate potential communication challenges and enhance overall compatibility.

3. Soul Urge Alignment:

- **Shared Desires:** Compatibility in Soul Urge Numbers indicates shared desires and motivations. Partners with aligned Soul Urge

Numbers, like 6, may prioritize family and nurturing, fostering emotional compatibility.

- **Navigating Differences:** Recognizing differences in Soul Urge Numbers allows couples to understand varying emotional needs and work towards a harmonious balance.

4. Overall Numerological Harmony:

- **Balanced Profiles:** A numerologically compatible couple often has a balance in their overall profiles, with complementary traits and shared goals.

- **Comprehensive Understanding:** Considering multiple aspects of numerology provides a more comprehensive understanding of compatibility, allowing couples to appreciate each other's strengths and navigate challenges.

5. Personal Growth Considerations:

- **Supportive Dynamics:** Numerology can highlight areas where individuals can support each other's personal growth. Compatible couples may encourage and inspire each other in their respective journeys.

- **Addressing Challenges:** Awareness of potential challenges based on numerology allows couples to proactively address issues, fostering a supportive and growth-oriented relationship.

Numerology offers a unique perspective on compatibility, providing a structured way to understand and appreciate the dynamics between individuals. While it's essential not to rely solely on numerology for relationship decisions, it can serve as a valuable tool for self-awareness and enhancing mutual understanding in partnerships.

Using Numerology in Daily Life

Numerology isn't just a peek into your future or a romantic compatibility test – it's a tool you can wield every day to navigate life with greater awareness and insight! Here are some ways to weave numerology into your daily routine:

1. Planning your day:

• Choose auspicious dates: Check online numerology calendars to identify dates with energies aligned with your goals. Plan important meetings, presentations, or creative endeavors for days that favor success and productivity.

• Personalize your day with numbers: Assign a number to each hour of the day based on your Life Path Number or current intentions. For example, a day focused on communication (Life Path 3) might have hour 3 dedicated to catching up with loved ones, hour 9 for creative brainstorming, and hour 18 for expressing yourself through writing.

2. Making decisions:

• Seek guidance from your numbers: When faced with a dilemma, look at the numerological meanings of the options. Consider choices that resonate with your Life Path, Soul Urge, or current challenges you're working on.

• Use Master Numbers as affirmations: Write down affirmations related to your goals and choose a corresponding Master Number (11 for intuition, 22 for mastery, 33 for unconditional love). Carry the affirmation with you or meditate on it during the day to attract the desired energy.

3. Cultivating personal growth:

• Track your Life Path cycles: Every nine years, your Life Path shifts, bringing new themes and challenges. Understanding these cycles can help you prepare for transitions and make conscious choices in alignment with your evolving goals.

• Identify your Karmic Debt Numbers: These numbers signify lessons you carry from past lives. Recognizing them allows you to work on overcoming negative tendencies and embracing your highest potential.

4. Enhancing relationships:

• Understand your partner's numbers: Learning your partner's Life Path, Expression, and Soul Urge Numbers can give you insights into their communication style, desires, and potential challenges. Use this knowledge to improve communication, build empathy, and navigate differences with greater understanding.

• Plan special dates based on compatible numbers: Choose anniversary dates, vacations, or even small outings based on number combinations that symbolize harmony, love, or shared goals.

Remember:

• Numerology is a tool, not a rulebook. Don't let numbers dictate your life; use them as guides to make informed choices and navigate situations with greater awareness.

• Focus on the positive potential of your numbers. Use them to attract opportunities, cultivate strengths, and overcome challenges.

• Keep an open mind and have fun! Experiment with different ways to incorporate numerology into your daily life and see how it enhances your journey.

So, go forth and weave the magic of numbers into your everyday tapestry! Numerology awaits to enrich your life with self-discovery, informed choices, and a deeper connection to your own personal story.

Numerology isn't just a mystical exploration of numbers; it can be a practical tool to enhance your daily life! Here are some ways to incorporate the wisdom of numbers into your routine:

Decision Making:

• Stuck between choices? Analyze the Life Path Numbers associated with each option. A new career path with a Life Path 4 might offer stability, while one with a Life Path 5 could be more adventurous. Choosing aligns with your core desires and purpose.

• Planning an important event? Check the numerological day and month. Auspicious days for business ventures (8), creative endeavors (3), or communication (5) can guide your scheduling.

Relationships:

• Want to understand a friend or partner better? Explore their Life Path Number and Expression Number. Learning their communication style and core desires can deepen your understanding and communication.

• Facing relationship challenges? Identify potential areas of conflict through numerological compatibility analysis. Understanding your differences can lead to more effective communication and conflict resolution.

Personal Growth:

• Feeling stuck in a rut? Examine your Soul Urge Number. It represents your deepest yearnings. aligning your daily activities and goals with these desires can bring fulfillment and purpose.

• Need a boost of motivation? Choose an affirmation aligned with your dominant numerological energies. For example, a Life Path 1 might use "I am confident and independent," while a Life Path 3 might say "I embrace joy and creativity."

Daily Rituals:

• Start your day with a numerology practice. Choose a lucky number based on the day or your Life Path and focus on its positive energy throughout the day.

• Use numerological mantras or affirmations. Repeating positive statements aligned with your numbers can boost confidence, attract desired outcomes, and enhance your mood.

Remember:

• Numerology is a tool, not a rulebook. Use it as a guide, not a rigid dictate.

• Personal awareness and intuition are crucial. Interpret numerological messages through the lens of your own experiences and feelings.

• Focus on the positive. Use numerology to identify strengths, potential, and opportunities for growth.

By incorporating these tips, you can infuse your daily life with a touch of numerological magic. Open yourself to the insights and possibilities that numbers offer, and watch your journey unfold with greater awareness, purpose, and a dash of cosmic guidance!

Feel free to ask me any further questions about using numerology in specific areas of your daily life. I'm here to support your journey of self-discovery and empowerment through the fascinating language of numbers!

Numerology, with its enchanting dance of numbers, can be more than just a fascinating exploration of your personality and potential. It can be a practical tool to navigate your daily life with greater awareness and purpose. Here are some ways you can incorporate numerology into your everyday routine:

Making Decisions:

• Identify lucky days: Based on your personal numerology chart, certain days hold higher vibrations for specific activities, like signing contracts (Life Path 8 day) or pursuing creative projects (Expression Number 3 day).

• Channel auspicious energies: Planning important meetings or presentations on days aligned with your Life Path or Expression Number can boost your confidence and attract positive outcomes.

• Use mantras and affirmations: Incorporate numerologically relevant numbers or phrases into your daily affirmations to attract desired energies, like "I am abundant and prosperous" on an 8 day.

Enhancing Relationships:

• Understanding compatibility: Numerology can offer insights into the strengths and potential challenges in your relationships with friends, family, or romantic partners.

• Improving communication: By understanding your and your partner's Expression Numbers, you can adjust your communication styles for better understanding and empathy.

• Celebrating special days: Birthdays, anniversaries, or other significant dates can be enhanced by choosing dates with numerologically positive vibrations for added joy and blessings.

Bringing Focus and Intention:

• Planning your day: Align your daily tasks with the energies of the day (e.g., creative tasks on a 3 day, analytical tasks on a 7 day).

• Setting intentions: Infuse your intentions for the day, week, or month with relevant numerological numbers to attract specific energies, like "abundance" for an 8 month or "harmony" for a 2 week.

• Choosing lucky charms: Wear or carry objects or symbols associated with your lucky numbers or Life Path to attract positive vibrations throughout the day.

Remember:

• Numerology is not a magic wand; it's a tool for self-awareness and conscious choice.

• Don't become overly reliant on numbers; trust your intuition and inner wisdom as well.

• Use numerology with a positive mindset and focus on its potential for growth and fulfillment.

By incorporating these practices into your daily life, you can harness the power of numerology to attract positive energy, make informed decisions, and navigate your relationships with greater understanding and harmony. So, embrace the magic of numbers, and let them guide you towards a life filled with purpose, joy, and personal growth!

Feel free to ask me any specific questions about applying numerology to your daily life or exploring the numerological significance of particular situations or events. I'm here to guide you on your journey of conscious living and empower you to use the wisdom of numbers to create a life you love!

Numerology isn't just a mystical exploration of numbers; it can be a practical tool to enhance your daily life! Here are some ways to incorporate the wisdom of numbers into your routine:

Decision Making:

• Stuck between choices? Analyze the Life Path Numbers associated with each option. A new career path with a Life Path 4 might offer stability, while one with a Life Path 5 could be more adventurous. Choosing aligns with your core desires and purpose.

• Planning an important event? Check the numerological day and month. Auspicious days for business ventures (8), creative endeavors (3), or communication (5) can guide your scheduling.

Relationships:

• Want to understand a friend or partner better? Explore their Life Path Number and Expression Number. Learning their communication style and core desires can deepen your understanding and communication.

• Facing relationship challenges? Identify potential areas of conflict through numerological compatibility analysis. Understanding your differences can lead to more effective communication and conflict resolution.

Personal Growth:

• Feeling stuck in a rut? Examine your Soul Urge Number. It represents your deepest yearnings. aligning your daily activities and goals with these desires can bring fulfillment and purpose.

• Need a boost of motivation? Choose an affirmation aligned with your dominant numerological energies. For example, a Life Path 1 might use "I am confident and independent," while a Life Path 3 might say "I embrace joy and creativity."

Daily Rituals:

• Start your day with a numerology practice. Choose a lucky number based on the day or your Life Path and focus on its positive energy throughout the day.

• Use numerological mantras or affirmations. Repeating positive statements aligned with your numbers can boost confidence, attract desired outcomes, and enhance your mood.

Remember:

• Numerology is a tool, not a rulebook. Use it as a guide, not a rigid dictate.

• Personal awareness and intuition are crucial. Interpret numerological messages through the lens of your own experiences and feelings.

• Focus on the positive. Use numerology to identify strengths, potential, and opportunities for growth.

By incorporating these tips, you can infuse your daily life with a touch of numerological magic. Open yourself to the insights and possibilities that numbers offer, and watch your journey unfold with greater awareness, purpose, and a dash of cosmic guidance!

Integrating numerology into daily life can be a fun and insightful way to gain a deeper understanding of yourself and make informed choices. Here are some simple ways to use numerology in your daily routine :

1. Life Path Number Reflection:

- **Morning Routine:** Start your day by reflecting on the characteristics of your Life Path Number. Consider how these traits can guide your approach to challenges and opportunities throughout the day.

2. Expression Number Awareness:

- **Communication Styles:** Be mindful of your Expression Number traits when interacting with others. Understanding your natural communication style and recognizing those of others can enhance effective communication.

3. Soul Urge Check-In:

- **Emotional Well-being:** Periodically check in with your Soul Urge Number to understand your emotional needs. Ensure that your daily choices align with your innermost desires for fulfillment and well-being.

4. Numerological Planning:

- **Key Dates:** Consider numerology when planning important events or making decisions. Pay attention to dates with significant numerological resonance for more favorable outcomes.

5. Daily Affirmations:

- **Positive Reinforcement:** Create daily affirmations based on your numerological insights. Affirmations that align with your Life Path or Expression Number can foster a positive mindset and motivation.

6. **Numerological Journaling:**

• **Reflections:** Keep a numerology journal to reflect on your experiences, decisions, and emotions. Note any patterns or connections between numerological aspects and daily events.

7. **Relationship Insights:**

• **Understanding Others:** Use numerology to understand the numerological profiles of friends, family, or colleagues. This can provide insights into their motivations and help improve relationships.

8. **Decision-Making Guide:**

• **Making Choices:** When faced with decisions, consider how your numerology numbers might influence your inclinations. This awareness can guide you toward choices aligned with your true self.

9. **Monthly Forecast:**

• **Planning Ahead:** At the beginning of each month, explore the numerological forecast for that period. This can offer insights into potential themes and energies, helping you plan activities and set intentions.

10. **Gratitude Practice:**

• **Numerology of Gratitude:** Express gratitude for the positive aspects associated with your numerology numbers. Recognize the strengths and opportunities that each number brings into your life.

By incorporating numerology into your daily life in these simple ways, you can enhance self-awareness, make more aligned choices, and foster a deeper connection with the surrounding energies. Remember, numerology is a tool for personal insight and growth, adding an extra layer of understanding to your daily experiences.

Navigating Your Career Path with the Power of Numerology

Choosing the right career path can be daunting, but numerology can offer a unique perspective to guide your decision. By understanding the energies associated with your Life Path Number, Expression Number, and Soul Urge Number, you can gain valuable insights into your strengths, potential pitfalls, and fulfilling career choices.

Life Path Number:

• Your core essence and life purpose. Identifying your Life Path Number can reveal your natural inclinations, talents, and the overall direction your career should take.

• For example: A Life Path 1 might thrive in leadership roles or entrepreneurial ventures, while a Life Path 5 might excel in dynamic, fast-paced fields like travel or marketing.

Expression Number:

• How you communicate and project yourself professionally. Understanding your Expression Number can help you choose a career where your communication style and skills are valued.

• For example: A person with an Expression Number 3 might shine in creative fields like writing or performing, while someone with an Expression Number 8 might excel in persuasive roles like sales or negotiations.

Soul Urge Number:

• Your deepest passions and desires. Aligning your career with your Soul Urge Number can lead to a fulfilling and meaningful work experience.

• For example: Someone with a Soul Urge Number 2 might find happiness in careers focused on collaboration and helping others, while someone with a Soul Urge Number 7 might thrive in research, analysis, or spiritual pursuits.

Matching Numbers to Careers:

• Life Path 1: Leadership, entrepreneurship, innovation, management

• Life Path 2: Diplomacy, cooperation, counseling, teaching, healthcare

• Life Path 3: Creativity, communication, entertainment, arts, marketing

• Life Path 4: Organization, practicality, engineering, finance, construction

• Life Path 5: Freedom, adaptability, travel, sales, communication

• Life Path 6: Nurturing, caregiving, teaching, social work, healthcare

• Life Path 7: Analysis, research, spirituality, philosophy, academia

• Life Path 8: Power, ambition, business, finance, politics, law

• Life Path 9: Humanitarianism, idealism, creativity, service, social work

Beyond the Numbers:

• Remember, numerology is a guide, not a guarantee. Your personal experiences, skills, and education also play a crucial role in your career success.

• Use numerology to identify your strengths and potential challenges. This can help you choose a career path where you can excel and find fulfillment.

• Don't be afraid to explore different options. Experimenting and trying new things can help you discover hidden talents and passions.

Numerology can be a powerful tool to navigate your career journey. By understanding the energies and messages hidden within your numbers

You can make informed choices, find your true calling, and embark on a fulfilling professional path.

1. **Life Path Number and Career Path:**

- **Identify Strengths:** Understand the traits associated with your Life Path Number. Identify strengths that align with certain career paths. For example, Life Path 8 individuals often excel in leadership and business roles.

- **Match Interests:** Consider career options that resonate with your natural interests and passions, which are reflected in your Life Path Number.

2. **Expression Number and Communication Skills:**

- **Communication Roles:** Your Expression Number reflects your communication style. If you have an Expression 3, you might thrive in roles that involve creativity and effective communication, such as writing, marketing, or public relations.

- **Creative Pursuits:** Explore careers that allow you to express your creative abilities and communicate effectively.

3. **Soul Urge Number and Career Satisfaction:**

- **Fulfilling Desires:** Your Soul Urge Number reveals your innermost desires. Consider how your career choices align with these desires for fulfillment and satisfaction.

- **Helping Professions:** If your Soul Urge is 9, you may find fulfillment in careers that involve helping others, such as counseling, social work, or humanitarian work.

4. Numerology in Decision-Making:

- **Choosing Dates:** Use numerology to choose favorable dates for important career decisions, interviews, or job changes. Consider dates that resonate positively with your personal numerology.

5. Harmony in Coworker Numerology:

- **Team Dynamics:** Understand the numerology of your coworkers or potential collaborators. Numerological harmony can contribute to positive team dynamics and collaborative efforts.

- **Conflict Resolution:** If conflicts arise, consider numerological insights to navigate and understand differing perspectives.

6. Timing Career Moves:

- **Personal Year Number:** Explore your Personal Year Number, which indicates the energy of the current year for you. Consider making significant career moves during a year that aligns with your goals.

7. Networking and Relationship Building:

- **Understanding Others:** Use numerology to understand the numerological profiles of colleagues or business partners. This can provide insights into their working styles and motivations.

- **Networking Events:** Choose numerologically favorable dates for networking events or business meetings to enhance positive interactions.

Remember, while numerology can provide guidance, it's just one factor to consider in making career decisions. Practical considerations, skills, and personal interests should also play a significant role in your professional choices. Numerology serves as a complementary tool for self-awareness and alignment with your true potential.

Harnessing Numerology for Personal Growth

Numerology isn't just about predicting the future or revealing compatibility; it's a potent tool for self-discovery and personal growth. By delving into the language of numbers, you can unlock hidden strengths, confront challenges, and chart a course towards your most fulfilling self. Here are some ways to harness the power of numerology for your own transformation:

Discover Your Core Essence:

• Life Path Number: This foundational number reveals your innate talents, life purpose, and the overarching challenges you're meant to overcome. Understanding your Life Path empowers you to make choices aligned with your true essence and navigate your journey with greater clarity.

• For example: A Life Path 3 might embrace their natural creativity and find purpose in expressing themselves through artistic pursuits, while a Life Path 8 might channel their ambition towards building impactful legacies in leadership roles.

Unmask Your Inner Voice:

• Soul Urge Number: This hidden number whispers your deepest desires, the passions that fuel your soul and motivate you from within. Aligning your life choices with your Soul Urge can lead to increased fulfillment and a sense of living authentically.

• For example: Someone with a Soul Urge Number 2 might prioritize nurturing relationships and seek careers in counseling or social work, while someone with a Soul Urge Number 5 might crave adventure and find happiness in travel or exploring new experiences.

Master Your Communication:

• Expression Number: This number represents your public persona, how you project yourself to the world, and your preferred communication style. Understanding your Expression Number can help you refine your communication skills, build stronger relationships, and assert yourself effectively.

• For example: A person with an Expression Number 1 might cultivate confidence and assertiveness to communicate their leadership qualities, while someone with an Expression Number 4 might focus on clear and concise communication to gain trust and build credibility.

Embrace Challenges as Opportunities:

• Identify areas for growth: Numerology doesn't shy away from challenges. Each number carries potential pitfalls and areas for improvement. Recognizing these can be the first step towards overcoming them.

• For example: A Life Path 7 might struggle with isolation and learn to find balance through connecting with others, while a Life Path 1 might confront their tendency towards dominance and cultivate teamwork and humility.

Practice Daily Rituals:

• Affirmations: Aligned with your dominant numerological energies, affirmations can boost your confidence, attract desired outcomes, and shift your mindset towards growth.

• Lucky Days: Choose auspicious days based on numerology for important events, business ventures, or creative endeavors. This can infuse your actions with a touch of cosmic synchronicity.

• Mantra repetition: Chanting mantras associated with your numbers can focus your intentions, tap into specific energies, and enhance your daily practice.

Remember:

• Numerology is a personal journey, not a rigid doctrine. Interpret its messages through your own intuition and experiences.

• Focus on the positive. Use numerology to identify your strengths, potential, and opportunities for growth.

• Embrace the ongoing journey. Personal growth is a continuous process, and numerology can be your guiding light along the way.

By tapping into the wisdom of numbers, you can unlock your true potential, overcome challenges, and embark on a journey of self-discovery that leads to a more fulfilling and empowered you. Feel free to explore specific questions you have about using numerology for your personal growth journey. I'm here to be your guide as you unlock the magic within your numbers!

Harnessing numerology for personal growth involves using the insights provided by your numerological profile to make informed choices and cultivate self-awareness. Here's how you can leverage numerology for personal development :

1. Understanding Your Numbers:

• **Study Your Numerology Profile:** Delve into the meanings associated with your Life Path, Expression, and Soul Urge Numbers. Understand the traits, strengths, and potential challenges associated with each number.

2. Setting Personal Goals:

• **Align Goals with Numerology:** Set personal goals that align with your numerological profile. Consider your innate strengths and desires when planning your objectives.

3. Daily Affirmations:

• **Positive Reinforcement:** Create daily affirmations based on your numerology insights. Affirmations that resonate with your Life Path or Expression Number can positively influence your mindset.

4. Reflecting on Challenges:

• **Numerological Insights during Challenges:** When facing challenges, reflect on how your numerology numbers may influence your approach. Use this awareness to navigate difficulties with a better understanding of your strengths.

5. Career Choices and Personal Fulfillment:

• **Aligning Career with Numerology:** Consider how your career choices align with your numerology numbers. Ensure that your professional pursuits resonate with your natural talents and passions.

6. Relationship Dynamics:

• **Numerological Insights in Relationships:** Apply numerology to understand your dynamics with others, whether in personal or professional relationships. Use this understanding, enhancing communication and mutual understanding.

7. Planning Major Life Changes:

• **Numerological Timing:** When contemplating major life changes, such as moving or starting a new venture, consider numerology for timing. Choose periods aligned with your Personal Year Number for added support.

8. Self-Reflection and Journaling:

• **Numerology Journal:** Maintain a numerology journal where you document your reflections, experiences, and observations. Use this journal for self-reflection and personal growth insights.

9. Building Resilience:

• **Challenges as Opportunities:** Embrace challenges as opportunities for growth, considering your numerological strengths. Use your numerology numbers as a guide to building resilience and overcoming obstacles.

10. Mindful Decision-Making:

• **Numerology in Decision-Making:** Incorporate numerology into your decision-making process. Whether it's choosing dates, making career decisions, or planning activities, use numerology for mindful and aligned choices.

Remember, while numerology provides valuable insights, personal growth is a holistic journey. Combine numerological awareness with other self-improvement practices to create a comprehensive approach to your well-being and development. Numerology serves as a guide, helping you tap into your inherent potential for personal growth and fulfillment.

Weaving the magic of numbers into your daily life

Weaving the magic of numbers into your daily life can be a transformative and empowering experience! Here are some ways to integrate numerology into your rituals, enriching your day with cosmic guidance and personal growth:

Morning Rituals:

• Set intentions: Start your day with an affirmation aligned with your numerology. For a Life Path 3, "I embrace creativity and joy" could be powerful. For a Life Path 8, "I manifest success and abundance" might resonate.

• Lucky Days: Schedule important meetings, presentations, or creative pursuits on numerologically auspicious days. Fridays (ruled by Venus) are ideal for artistic endeavors, while Thursdays (ruled by Jupiter) favor expansion and success.

• Number meditation: Focus on your core Life Path Number, visualizing its energy surrounding you. This can bring clarity and purpose to your day.

Throughout the Day:

• Mantras: Choose a short mantra aligned with your dominant numerology energies and repeat it throughout the day. "I am confident" for a Life Path 1 or "I am compassionate" for a Life Path 6 can shift your mindset and attract positive energy.

• Numerology breaks: Take short breaks throughout the day to reflect on a specific number. Consider its meaning in your current situation or meditate on its associated qualities.

• Gratitude practice: Before bedtime, write down five things you're grateful for, each associated with a different numerology vibration. For example, gratitude for "love" (6) and "creativity" (3).

Evening Rituals:

• Numerology journal: Reflect on your day through the lens of numbers. Did you encounter challenges associated with your Life Path number? Did you experience synchronicities with your Expression Number?

• Numerology oracle cards: Draw a numerology oracle card each evening for guidance and insights. Interpret its message within the context of your current journey.

• Visualization: Visualize your goals and desires infused with the energy of specific numbers. Imagine achieving success (8) surrounded by abundance (6) or radiating creativity (3) in your artistic pursuits.

Remember:

• Personalize your rituals. Experiment and find practices that resonate with you and your numerological needs.

• Focus on consistency. The more you integrate numerology into your daily routine, the deeper its impact will be.

• Openness is key. Be receptive to the subtle messages and guidance numbers offer throughout your day.

By weaving numerology into your daily rituals, you can cultivate a deeper connection to yourself, attract positive energy, and navigate your journey with greater awareness and purpose. So, start small, experiment, and watch as the magic of numbers unfolds in your daily life!

Integrating numerology into daily rituals

Integrating numerology into daily rituals can add a meaningful and reflective dimension to your routine. Here's a simple guide on how to incorporate numerology into your daily life :

1. Morning Reflection:

- **Start with Your Life Path Number:** Begin your day by reflecting on the traits associated with your Life Path Number. Consider how these characteristics can guide your actions and mindset for the day.

2. Daily Affirmations:

- **Align with Expression Number:** Create daily affirmations that resonate with your Expression Number. These affirmations can reinforce positive communication styles and creative energies throughout the day.

3. Numerological Planning:

- **Choose Dates Mindfully:** When scheduling appointments, meetings, or significant activities, choose dates that align with your numerology for a more harmonious and positive experience.

4. Midday Check-In:

- **Connect with Soul Urge:** Take a moment in the middle of the day to check in with your Soul Urge Number. Reflect on whether your actions and choices align with your innermost desires for fulfillment.

5. Creative Breaks:

- **Expression Number Breaks:** If possible, schedule short breaks during the day to engage in activities that align with your Expression Number, fostering creativity and self-expression.

6. Evening Reflection:

- **Review Your Numbers:** Reflect on your numerology numbers in the evening. Consider how your actions and experiences throughout the day align with your Life Path, Expression, and Soul Urge Numbers.

7. Numerological Journaling:

- **Document Daily Observations:** Maintain a numerology journal to document your daily observations, experiences, and feelings. This practice can deepen your self-awareness and provide insights over time.

8. Bedtime Affirmations:

- **Align with Soul Urge:** End your day with bedtime affirmations that resonate with your Soul Urge Number. Focus on affirmations that reinforce your innermost desires and bring a sense of peace.

9. Dream Interpretation:

- **Numerological Themes in Dreams:** Pay attention to any recurring numerological themes in your dreams. These may offer additional insights into your subconscious thoughts and feelings.

10. Weekly Numerology Check:

- **Plan for the Week:** At the beginning of each week, review your numerology forecast for guidance. Use this information to plan your activities and set intentions for the upcoming week.

By incorporating numerology into your daily rituals, you infuse your routine with intentional and mindful practices. This can deepen your connection with your true self and provide a framework for making choices that align with your inherent traits and desires.

Numerology and Decision-Making

A Compass for Your Choices

Numerology can be a powerful tool for navigating the sometimes-treacherous waters of decision-making. By understanding the energies associated with your Life Path Number, Expression Number, and Soul Urge Number, you can gain valuable insights into potential outcomes and align your choices with your deeper desires and purpose.

Here's how numerology can guide your decision-making:

1. Awareness of Your Core Values:

• Life Path Number: This number reveals your core essence, strengths, and life purpose. Understanding your Life Path helps you identify decisions that align with your values and overall direction in life. For instance, a Life Path 3 might be drawn to creative pursuits, while a Life Path 8 might prioritize career advancement and leadership roles.

2. Recognizing Obstacles and Opportunities:

• Numerology can highlight potential challenges and opportunities associated with each option. For example, a Life Path 4 might be drawn to a stable job but might need to consider its potential for growth and fulfillment. A Life Path 5 might crave adventure, but might need to balance it with the need for security and stability.

3. Intuitive Guidance through Challenges:

• Soul Urge Number: This hidden number whispers your deepest desires and yearnings. Aligning your decisions with your Soul Urge can lead to a more fulfilling life, even if it means facing challenges. For instance, someone with a Soul Urge Number 2 might be drawn to a career in counseling despite initial fears of stepping outside their comfort zone.

4. Communication and Collaboration:

• Expression Number: This number reveals your communication style and how you project yourself to the world. Understanding your own and others' Expression Numbers can help you communicate effectively and collaborate with different personalities, leading to better decision-making in group settings.

5. Beyond the Numbers:

• Numerology is a tool, not a rule book. It should be used in conjunction with your own intuition, critical thinking, and consideration of external factors.

• Focus on the positive. Use numerology to identify strengths, opportunities, and potential areas for growth in your choices.

• Embrace the journey. Life is full of decisions, and numerology can help you navigate them with greater awareness and purpose.

Remember:

• There is no single "right" answer. Numerology helps you understand the potential consequences of your choices and make decisions aligned with your deeper self.

• Be open to revising your decisions as you gain more information and your perspective evolves.

• Trust your intuition and combine it with the insights numerology offers to chart your own unique path.

1. Understanding Your Life Path Number:

> • **Reflect on Traits:** Before making a decision, reflect on the traits associated with your Life Path Number. Consider how these qualities may influence your approach to the decision at hand.

2. Expression Number and Communication:

- **Evaluate Communication Styles:** Your Expression Number reflects your communication style. Assess how your communication preferences may impact the decision-making process, especially in collaborative situations.

3. Soul Urge Number and Personal Desires:

- **Consider Inner Desires:** Check your Soul Urge Number to understand your innermost desires. Ensure that your decision aligns with these desires for personal fulfillment.

4. Numerological Timing:

- **Choose Numerologically Favorable Dates:** When possible, choose dates for making decisions that align with your numerology. This could involve considering your Personal Year Number or selecting dates with numerological resonance.

5. Aligning with Expression in Career Decisions:

- **Career Choices:** When making career-related decisions, consider how your Expression Number aligns with the nature of the role or industry. Ensure that your decisions resonate with your natural talents and interests.

6. Personal Year Number for Timely Decisions:

- **Timely Decisions:** Your Personal Year Number provides insights into the energy of the current year for you. Consider making important decisions during a year that aligns with your goals and intentions.

7. Consulting Your Numerology Chart:

- **Chart Analysis:** If faced with a complex decision, consult your entire numerology chart, including Life Path, Expression, and Soul

Urge Numbers. This holistic view can offer a more comprehensive understanding of your tendencies.

8. Numerological Insights in Relationships:

- **Consider Relationship Dynamics:** If your decision involves others, consider the numerology of those involved. Understanding the numerology of individuals can provide insights into potential dynamics and challenges.

9. Reflecting on Challenges Based on Numbers:

- **Anticipate Challenges:** Use your numerology insights to anticipate potential challenges associated with specific numbers. This awareness can help you navigate difficulties more effectively.

10. Revisit Numerology Journal:

- **Review Past Observations:** If you maintain a numerology journal, revisit past observations related to decision-making. Reflecting on your experiences can offer valuable lessons for future choices.

Numerology serves as a complementary tool in decision-making, providing a unique lens through which to view your traits, desires, and potential challenges. While it's essential to consider practical aspects and other factors, incorporating numerology can add an insightful layer to your decision-making process.

Here are examples of using numerology for guidance in various aspects of life:

Career:

• Choosing a career path: A Life Path 3 might thrive in creative fields like writing or performing, while a Life Path 8 might excel in business or leadership roles.

• Navigating job changes: Numerology can help identify potential challenges and opportunities in new positions, aligning them with your core values and strengths.

• Understanding work relationships: Knowing your Expression Number and those of your colleagues can improve communication and collaboration.

Relationships:

• Compatibility analysis: Explore potential harmony or challenges between Life Path Numbers to understand dynamics and areas for growth.

• Improving communication: Understanding your Expression Number and your partner's can lead to better communication styles and conflict resolution.

• Finding a fulfilling partnership: Aligning your Soul Urge Numbers with your partner's can create a deeper connection and shared goals.

Personal Growth:

• Identifying strengths and weaknesses: Numerology can reveal areas for improvement and opportunities to harness your natural talents.

• Overcoming challenges: Understanding the challenges associated with your Life Path Number can help you develop strategies to address them.

• Setting goals: Align your goals with your numerological energies to increase motivation and success.

Decision-Making:

• Weighing options: Analyze the Life Path Numbers associated with different choices to gain insights into potential outcomes and alignment with your purpose.

• Recognizing obstacles and opportunities: Numerology can highlight potential challenges and opportunities within each option, aiding in informed decisions.

• Trusting intuition: Listen to your Soul Urge Number's guidance, balancing logic with inner wisdom.

Daily Life:

• Choosing auspicious days: Schedule important events or activities on days aligned with numerology for potential success and harmony.

• Setting intentions and affirmations: Use affirmations aligned with your Life Path or Soul Urge Number to focus desires and attract positive energy.

• Finding personal power numbers: Identify lucky numbers or power numbers to tap into their energy and boost confidence.

Remember: Numerology is best used as a tool for self-awareness, not as a definitive predictor of the future. It offers insights and perspectives to guide your choices, but ultimately, your intuition, experiences, and personal growth play a vital role in shaping your journey.

Common Numerology Myths Debunked

Let's debunk some common numerology myths in a straightforward and easy-to-understand manner :

1. Myth: Numerology Predicts the Future

- **Debunked:** Numerology doesn't predict the future. It offers insights into your traits and tendencies, guiding self-discovery. While it can suggest favorable times for certain activities, it doesn't foresee specific events.

2. Myth: Numerology Is Only for Mystic Believers

- **Debunked:** Numerology is a tool for self-awareness, not exclusive to mysticism. People from various backgrounds find value in understanding their inherent traits and making informed choices based on numerological insights.

3. Myth: Numerology Is a Form of Magic

- **Debunked:** Numerology is not magic. It's a system that assigns meaning to numbers and their influence on individuals. It's a methodical and symbolic approach to understanding aspects of one's personality.

4. Myth: Numerology Is Only for Certain Cultures

- **Debunked:** Numerology is present in various cultures globally, each with its unique interpretations. It's not confined to a specific culture or belief system; different societies have embraced numerological concepts throughout history.

5. Myth: Numerology Can Change Your Destiny

- **Debunked:** Numerology offers insights, but it doesn't alter destiny. Personal agency, choices, and external factors also play crucial roles in shaping one's life. Numerology provides guidance but doesn't dictate outcomes.

6. Myth: Numerology Can Solve All Problems

- **Debunked:** Numerology is a tool for self-reflection, not a solution to all problems. It can offer insights, but practical actions, critical thinking, and addressing challenges actively are essential for problem-solving.

7. Myth: Numerology Is a New Age Trend

- **Debunked:** Numerology has ancient roots, dating back centuries. It's not a modern trend but has been used in various forms by cultures worldwide for a long time.

8. Myth: Numerology Can Tell You Everything About a Person

- **Debunked:** Numerology provides insights into certain aspects of personality, but it doesn't reveal every detail about a person. Individuals are complex, and numerology is just one lens through which to understand them.

9. Myth: Numerology Requires Special Powers

- **Debunked:** Anyone can learn and apply numerology. It doesn't require special powers or mystical abilities. Numerology is accessible to those interested in exploring its concepts.

10. Myth: Numerology Is Strictly Mathematical

- **Debunked:** While numerology involves assigning numerical values, its interpretations are symbolic and subjective. It blends mathematical principles with symbolic meanings to create a system for understanding traits and tendencies.

Understanding these debunked myths can provide a clearer perspective on what numerology is and isn't, dispelling misconceptions and allowing for a more informed approach to this fascinating tool of self-discovery.

Astrology and numerology

Astrology and numerology are distinct yet interconnected systems that people often use for self-discovery and understanding various aspects of their lives. Here's a brief exploration of both :

1. Astrology:

- **Basics:** Astrology is the study of the positions and movements of celestial bodies, such as planets and stars, and their potential influence on human affairs and natural events.

- **Components:** Astrology typically involves creating a natal (birth) chart based on the individual's date, time, and place of birth. This chart details the positions of the sun, moon, planets, and other celestial elements at the time of birth.

- **Signs and Houses:** Astrology divides the sky into 12 zodiac signs and houses. Each sign and house is associated with specific characteristics, traits, and areas of life.

2. Numerology:

- **Basics:** Numerology is the study of the symbolic meanings of numbers and their potential influence on individuals and events.

- **Components:** Numerology often involves calculating key numbers, such as the Life Path Number (derived from the date of birth), Expression Number (related to the full name), and Soul Urge Number (linked to vowels in the name).

- **Meanings:** Each number in numerology carries specific meanings and characteristics. Numerologists interpret these numbers to provide insights into personality traits, life path, and potential challenges.

3. **Interconnections:**

• **Personal Exploration:** Individuals often explore both astrology and numerology for a more comprehensive understanding of themselves. While astrology looks at celestial influences, numerology delves into the symbolism of numbers.

• **Combined Insights:** Combining insights from both systems can provide a multifaceted view of one's personality, strengths, and challenges.

4. **Applications:**

• **Astrological Applications:** Astrology is commonly used for predicting future trends, understanding compatibility in relationships, and gaining insights into personal strengths and challenges.

• **Numerological Applications:** Numerology is applied in self-discovery, decision-making, and understanding the influences of specific numbers on one's life.

5. **Different Philosophies:**

• **Astrological Philosophy:** Astrology is based on the idea that celestial bodies influence life on Earth, and the positions of these bodies at the time of birth can offer insights into an individual's personality and destiny.

• **Numerological Philosophy:** Numerology operates on the belief that numbers carry specific energies and vibrations that can influence an individual's experiences and characteristics.

In summary, astrology and numerology are complementary systems that provide unique perspectives on self-discovery. Exploring both can offer a more comprehensive understanding of oneself, allowing individuals to navigate life with greater awareness and insight. Whether you resonate more with celestial influences or the symbolism of numbers, both astrology and numerology provide valuable tools for personal growth and exploration.

Charts and arrows

In numerology, the terms "charts" and "arrows" are commonly associated with specific calculations and interpretations. Let's explore these concepts in a simplified manner :

1. **Numerology Charts:**

 • **Purpose:** Numerology charts are visual representations of the numerical values associated with specific aspects of an individual's life.

 • **Key Components:**

 • *Life Path Chart:* Represents the Life Path Number, calculated from the date of birth.

 • *Expression Chart:* Reflects the Expression Number, derived from the full name.

 • *Soul Urge Chart:* Illustrates the Soul Urge Number, calculated from the vowels in the full name.

 • **Interpretation:** Numerologists use these charts to interpret and communicate the meanings associated with different numbers, offering insights into personality traits and life paths.

2. **Numerology Arrows:**

 • **Purpose:** Numerology arrows are symbolic combinations of numbers within a chart that highlight specific aspects of an individual's life.

 • **Key Arrows:**

• *Arrow of Determination:* Focuses on the Life Path Number and its positioning in the chart, indicating determination and focus.

• *Arrow of Intellect:* Involves the Expression Number, showcasing intellectual abilities and communication skills.

• *Arrow of the Soul:* Centers around the Soul Urge Number, emphasizing desires and motivations.

• **Interpretation:** Numerologists analyze these arrows to provide nuanced insights into an individual's strengths and potential challenges.

In essence, numerology charts and arrows are tools used by practitioners to organize and interpret numerical data associated with an individual's birth date and name. These visual representations help convey the significance of specific numbers and their roles in shaping various aspects of one's personality and life path. Exploring these charts and arrows can offer a more detailed and personalized understanding of the influences of numerology on an individual.

Tarot and numerology

Tarot and numerology are two distinct yet interconnected systems often used for divination and self-discovery. Let's explore their relationship in simple terms :

1. Tarot Cards:

- **Purpose:** Tarot is a system of divination that uses a deck of cards to gain insights into the past, present, and future. Each card in the deck has symbolic imagery and meanings.

- **Components:** A standard tarot deck consists of 78 cards, divided into the Major Arcana (22 cards with significant life themes) and the Minor Arcana (56 cards resembling a regular playing card deck).

- **Numerology in Tarot:** Each card in the Major and Minor Arcana is associated with a specific number, contributing to its symbolism and interpretation.

2. Numerology in Tarot:

- **Major Arcana Numbers:** Cards in the Major Arcana are often numbered from 0 to 21. Numerology plays a role in understanding the significance of these numbers. For example, The Fool is associated with 0, representing potential and new beginnings.

- **Minor Arcana Numbers:** The Minor Arcana cards (Wands, Cups, Swords, Pentacles) are numbered from Ace to 10. Numerology influences the interpretation of these cards based on their assigned numbers.

3. Numerology and Card Interpretation:

• **Life Path and Tarot:** Some practitioners integrate numerology into tarot readings by considering an individual's Life Path Number in conjunction with the cards drawn. This adds a personalized layer to the interpretation.

• **Number Symbolism:** Numerology provides symbolic meanings for each number, influencing the interpretation of the cards. For instance, the number 3 might signify creativity and growth.

4. Combining Systems:

• **Holistic Approach:** Many individuals who explore both tarot and numerology take a holistic approach, combining insights from both systems. This involves interpreting the symbolism of the cards along with the numerological significance of the associated numbers.

5. Personal Exploration:

• **Self-Discovery:** Both tarot and numerology can be used for self-discovery. Individuals may use tarot cards alongside numerology to gain insights into their personalities, life paths, and potential outcomes.

In summary, tarot and numerology are interconnected through the symbolic meanings assigned to numbers in tarot cards. The integration of numerology into tarot readings adds depth and personalization to the interpretation, offering individuals a unique way to explore their lives and gain insights into various aspects of their existence.

Cornerstone

In numerology, terms like "cornerstone," "capstone," and "first vowel" are associated with specific components of a person's name, each contributing to the overall interpretation of their numerological profile. Let's break down these concepts in a simple and easy-to-understand manner :

1. Cornerstone:

- **Definition:** The cornerstone is the first letter of your first name. It represents the foundation of your personality and sets the tone for how you approach life.

- **Calculation:** Identify the first letter of your first name, and its corresponding numerical value is used in numerological analysis.

- **Significance:** The cornerstone provides insights into your basic nature and approach to challenges. It reflects the essence of your character.

2. Capstone:

- **Definition:** The capstone is the last letter of your first name. It symbolizes completion and the culmination of your efforts and experiences.

- **Calculation:** Identify the last letter of your first name, and its corresponding numerical value is used in numerological analysis.

- **Significance:** The capstone indicates how you bring projects to a close, your ability to finish what you start, and the manner in which you conclude various aspects of your life.

3. First Vowel:

- **Definition:** The first vowel is the initial vowel in your first name. It carries specific energetic qualities and influences your inner self.

- **Calculation:** Identify the first vowel in your first name, and its corresponding numerical value is used in numerological analysis.

- **Significance:** The first vowel provides insights into your deeper, more emotional self. It reflects aspects of your personality that may not be immediately apparent to others.

Understanding your cornerstone, capstone, and first vowel in numerology involves identifying the numerical values associated with the letters in your first name and considering their individual meanings. These components add layers of insight to your numerological profile, offering a more nuanced understanding of your character and tendencies.

Keep in mind that numerology is a symbolic system, and interpretations can vary. Exploring these elements can be a fun way to delve into the symbolic meanings associated with different aspects of your name.

The secret hidden in your name

The secrets hidden in your name, as explored through numerology, reveal insights into your personality, tendencies, and potential life path. Let's simplify this concept in a way that's easy to understand :

1. **Numerological Analysis:**

   • **Numbers and Letters:** In numerology, each letter of the alphabet is assigned a numerical value. These values are used to analyze and interpret the hidden meanings in your name.

   • **Key Components:** The cornerstone, capstone, and first vowel, as well as the overall numerical value of your name, contribute to the analysis.

2. **Cornerstone, Capstone, and First Vowel:**

   • **Cornerstone:** The first letter of your name represents your basic nature and how you approach life.

   • **Capstone:** The last letter of your name symbolizes completion, indicating how you conclude tasks and experiences.

   • **First Vowel:** The initial vowel in your name reflects your deeper, emotional self, offering insights beyond surface characteristics.

3. **Overall Numerical Value:**

   • **Calculation:** By assigning numerical values to each letter in your name and adding them together, you get the overall numerical value of your name.

- **Significance:** This total value is then interpreted to provide insights into your life path, personality traits, and potential challenges.

4. Life Path and Personality Traits:

- **Life Path Number:** Calculated from the overall numerical value of your name, the Life Path Number indicates your potential life journey and the traits you may exhibit.

- **Personality Traits:** Specific numbers associated with letters in your name contribute to the interpretation of your personality characteristics.

5. Self-Reflection and Awareness:

- **Understanding Yourself:** Exploring the secrets hidden in your name through numerology is a way to enhance self-awareness. It offers a different perspective on your character, motivations, and potential strengths.

6. Practical Applications:

- **Decision-Making:** Some people use numerology to inform decision-making and gain insights into their compatibility with others.

- **Self-Discovery:** The exploration of the secrets in your name can be a fun and insightful way to discover more about yourself and your unique qualities.

Remember, while numerology is an intriguing tool for self-discovery, its interpretations are subjective, and personal experiences play a significant role in shaping individual personalities. Exploring the secrets in your name through numerology can be a lighthearted and interesting way to gain additional insights into your own character.

How to find the secret hidden in your name

Discovering the secrets hidden in your name through numerology involves a few simple steps. Here's a straightforward guide :

1. Assign Numerical Values:

• **Use a Numerology Chart:** Assign numerical values to each letter of the alphabet. Common systems include A=1, B=2, C=3, and so on.

• **Write Down Your Name:** List each letter of your name and its corresponding numerical value.

2. Calculate Cornerstone, Capstone, and First Vowel:

• **Cornerstone:** Identify the first letter of your name and note its numerical value.

• **Capstone:** Find the last letter of your name and determine its numerical value.

• **First Vowel:** Locate the first vowel in your name and assign its numerical value.

3. Calculate Overall Numerical Value:

• **Add the Numbers:** Add up the numerical values of all the letters in your name to find the overall numerical value.

4. Life Path Number:

• **Reduce to a Single Digit:** If your overall numerical value is a two-digit number, reduce it to a single digit by adding the digits together.

- **Life Path Number:** This single-digit result is your Life Path Number, which offers insights into your potential life journey and characteristics.

5. Explore Individual Number Meanings:

- **Consult Numerology Meanings:** Look up the meanings associated with individual numbers in numerology. Each number carries specific traits and characteristics.

6. Reflect on Cornerstone, Capstone, and First Vowel:

- **Cornerstone:** Consider how the first letter reflects your basic nature and approach to life.

- **Capstone:** Reflect on the last letter and how it symbolizes the completion of tasks and experiences.

- **First Vowel:** Explore the emotional and deeper aspects represented by the first vowel.

7. Personal Reflection:

- **Consider Your Traits:** Reflect on how the numerological interpretations align with your personal experiences and traits.

- **Explore Challenges:** Consider potential challenges and growth opportunities suggested by the numerological insights.

8. Repeat for Different Names:

- **Explore Full Name:** Repeat the process for your full name, including your first, middle, and last names, to gain a more comprehensive understanding.

Remember, numerology is a symbolic system, and interpretations can vary. This exploration is meant to be a fun and introspective way to learn more about yourself. The secrets hidden in your name through numerology provide unique insights into your personality and can contribute to your journey of self-discovery.

The Destiny Numbers

The Destiny Number is often associated with the full name given at birth. Each letter of the alphabet is assigned a numerical value, and the Destiny Number is calculated by adding these values for all the letters in the full name. Here's a basic guide:

1. **Assign Numerical Values:**

   • Use a numerology chart to assign numerical values to each letter of the alphabet. Common systems include A=1, B=2, C=3, and so on.

2. **Write Down Your Full Birth Name:**

   • List each letter of your full birth name (as it appears on official documents).

3. **Assign Numerical Values to Each Letter:**

   • Assign the numerical values to each letter according to the numerology chart.

4. **Calculate the Destiny Number:**

   • Add up the numerical values of all the letters in your full name.

5. **Reduce to a Single Digit:**

   • If the result is a two-digit number, add the digits together to reduce it to a single digit.

6. **Interpret the Destiny Number:**

- Consult numerology resources to understand the meaning associated with your Destiny Number. Each number is believed to carry specific traits and characteristics.

For example, if your full name is JOHN SMITH:

- J=1, O=6, H=8, N=5

- S=1, M=4, I=9, T=2, H=8

Add these values: $1 + 6 + 8 + 5 + 1 + 4 + 9 + 2 + 8 = 44$

Reduce to a single digit: $4 + 4 = 8$

In this example, the Destiny Number would be 8, and you would then explore the numerological interpretations associated with the number 8.

Remember that numerology is a symbolic system, and interpretations may vary. It's often used as a tool for self-discovery and reflection.

To discover the meaning of your Destiny Number, simply follow these steps:

1. Write down your full birth name: This includes your first, middle, and last names.
2. Assign a numerical value to each letter: $A = 1$, $B = 2$, $C = 3$, and so on until $Z = 26$. You can find various tables online to reference if needed.
3. Reduce each set of two digits to a single digit: If you get a double-digit number like 17, add its digits together $(1 + 7)$ to get a single digit (8). Exceptions are master numbers 11 and 22, which you should keep as they hold their own special meanings.
4. Add up all the single digits: Once you have a single digit for each name component, add them all together.
5. Reduce the final sum to a single digit (except master numbers): If you get a double-digit number again, repeat step 3 by adding its digits together. Again, remember to keep master numbers 11 and 22.

The final single digit (or master number) you reach is your Destiny Number!

Once you have your Destiny Number, you can look up its meaning in various numerology resources. Each number carries unique attributes, talents, potential challenges, and life lessons. Knowing your Destiny Number can offer valuable insights into your purpose, career path, relationships, and overall fulfillment in life.

If you'd like, I can provide you with specific resources to explore the meaning of your Destiny Number based on various numerology schools and interpretations. Just let me know your number and any areas you'd like to learn more about!

Remember, numerology is a personal journey. Embrace its insights with an open mind and use them to empower your growth and self-discovery.

Choosing a baby's name in numerology

Choosing a baby's name in numerology involves considering the numerical values associated with each letter in the name to determine the potential traits and characteristics linked to those numbers. Here's a simplified guide on how to choose a baby's name in numerology:

1. **Assign Numerical Values:**

   - Use a numerology chart to assign numerical values to each letter of the alphabet. Common systems include A=1, B=2, C=3, and so on.

2. **Compile a List of Names:**

   - Create a list of names you are considering for your baby.

3. **Calculate Numerical Values:**

   - Assign the numerical values to each letter in the names on your list.

4. **Calculate Life Path Number:**

   - Add up the numerical values of all the letters in each name.

   - If the result is a two-digit number, reduce it to a single digit by adding the digits together.

5. **Consider Numerological Meanings:**

   - Research the meanings associated with each Life Path Number. Each number is believed to carry specific traits and characteristics.

6. **Check Compatibility:**

- Consider the compatibility of the baby's potential name with your last name and the overall sound of the name.

7. Reflect on Personal Preferences:

- Reflect on your personal preferences, cultural considerations, and any significance attached to certain names in your family or heritage.

8. Balance the Energies:

- Aim for a balanced name that aligns with positive traits while considering potential challenges associated with specific numbers.

9. Choose a Name with Positive Associations:

- Select a name that resonates positively with you and your family.

10. Seek Guidance if Necessary:

- If you're unsure or want additional insights, consider consulting with a numerologist or using online tools that provide detailed numerology readings.

Remember that while numerology can offer insights, the choice of a baby's name is a personal decision that involves various factors, including cultural, familial, and individual preferences. Numerology is just one tool among many that people use to bring meaning to the naming process. Ultimately, choose a name that feels right for you and your family.

The Soul Urge Number

In numerology, the Soul Urge Number, also known as the Heart's Desire Number, reflects your innermost desires, motivations, and the aspects of your personality that you hold most dear. To find your Soul Urge Number, follow these steps:

1. **Assign Numerical Values:**

    • Use a numerology chart to assign numerical values to each vowel in your full birth name (the name on your birth certificate). Common systems include A=1, E=5, I=9, O=6, U=3, and Y is sometimes considered a vowel.

2. **Write Down Your Full Name:**

    • List each vowel in your full birth name and assign the corresponding numerical value.

3. **Calculate Numerical Values:**

    • Add up the numerical values of all the vowels in your full birth name.

4. **Reduce to a Single Digit:**

    • If the result is a two-digit number, reduce it to a single digit by adding the digits together.

5. **Interpret the Soul Urge Number:**

    • Consult numerology resources to understand the meaning associated with your Soul Urge Number. Each number is believed to carry specific traits and characteristics.

For example, if your full birth name is JOHN SMITH:

- O=6

- I=9

Add these values: 6 + 9 = 15

Reduce to a single digit: 1 + 5 = 6

In this example, the Soul Urge Number would be 6. You would then explore the numerological interpretations associated with the number 6.

Your Soul Urge Number provides insights into your deepest desires and motivations. It represents the qualities and characteristics that you value at a profound level. Understanding this number can offer valuable insights into aspects of yourself that may not be immediately apparent.

Keep in mind that numerology is a symbolic system, and interpretations may vary.

How to find and what is my personal number

In numerology, your Personal Year Number represents the energy and experiences you are likely to encounter during a specific year. To calculate your Personal Year Number, follow these steps:

1. **Know Your Birthdate:**

   • The calculation is based on your birthdate, specifically the day and month.

2. **Assign Numerical Values:**

   • Assign numerical values to the day and month of your birth using a numerology chart. For example, January (1) would be 1, February (2) would be 2, and so on. If your birthdate is November 23, the day value is 23.

3. **Calculate the Universal Year Number:**

   • Determine the Universal Year Number for the current year. This is a broader energy that affects everyone and is calculated by adding the digits of the current year together and reducing to a single digit. For example, for the year 2023, calculate 2 + 0 + 2 + 3 = 7.

4. **Add Your Birthdate to the Universal Year Number:**

   • Add the numerical values of your birthdate (day and month) to the Universal Year Number. For example, if your birthdate is November 23, and the Universal Year Number is 7 (as in the example above), you would calculate 11 (November) + 23 (day) + 7 (Universal Year) = 41.

5. **Reduce to a Single Digit:**

• If the result is a two-digit number, reduce it to a single digit by adding the digits together. Using the example above, $4 + 1 = 5$.

6. Interpret Your Personal Year Number:

• Consult numerology resources to understand the meaning associated with your Personal Year Number. Each number is believed to carry specific energy and themes.

Your Personal Year Number provides insights into the experiences and challenges you may encounter during a specific year. Each number is associated with different energies, and understanding your Personal Year can help you navigate and make the most of the opportunities that come your way.

In numerology, the Soul Urge Number (also known as the Heart's Desire Number) and the Personality Number are essential components that offer insights into different aspects of an individual's character. Here's a brief overview of the meanings associated with these numbers:

1. Soul Urge Number:

- **Calculation:** The Soul Urge Number is derived from the vowels in your full birth name. Each vowel is assigned a numerical value, and the values are added to find the Soul Urge Number.

- **Meaning:** The Soul Urge Number represents your innermost desires, motivations, and the aspects of your personality that are deeply important to you. It reflects what you truly want in life at a profound level.

- **Interpretation:** Each number from 1 to 9 carries specific traits, and the interpretation of your Soul Urge Number involves understanding the characteristics associated with that particular number. For example, a Soul Urge Number of 3 may indicate a deep desire for self-expression, creativity, and joy.

2. Personality Number:

- **Calculation:** The Personality Number is derived from the consonants in your full birth name. Each consonant is assigned a numerical value, and the values are added to find the Personality Number.

- **Meaning:** The Personality Number represents the outward expression of yourself, the image you project to the world, and the characteristics others may see in you. It reflects the social mask you wear.

- **Interpretation:** Similar to the Soul Urge Number, the Personality Number is associated with specific traits based on the numerical values. Understanding your Personality Number can provide insights into how you present yourself to others. For instance, a Personality Number of 5 may suggest adaptability, curiosity, and a love for freedom.

Keep in mind that numerology is a symbolic system, and interpretations may vary. It's often used as a tool for self-reflection and personal insight. The meanings associated with these numbers are broad guidelines, and individual experiences may differ.

If you're interested in discovering your Soul Urge Number and Personality Number, you can share the vowels and consonants in your full birth name, respectively, and I can assist you with the calculations and interpretations.

Understanding Maturity Numbers

Introduction:

In this chapter, we delve into the fascinating realm of Maturity Numbers, key elements in numerology that offer a glimpse into the evolving nature of an individual's personality over time. As we explore each Maturity Number, readers will gain valuable insights into the traits and focal points that may shape their personal development.

Maturity Number 1:

Traits: Independence, leadership, assertiveness. **Focus:** Developing self-confidence and taking initiative.

Explanation: The Maturity Number 1 signifies a journey towards self-discovery and leadership. Individuals with this number may find their later years marked by a strong sense of independence and a desire to take charge of their lives.

Maturity Number 2:

Traits: Cooperation, diplomacy, sensitivity. **Focus:** Nurturing relationships and creating harmony.

Explanation: Maturity Number 2 reflects the importance of relationships and harmony. Readers will discover how fostering cooperation and cultivating sensitivity can lead to fulfilling connections in their mature years.

Maturity Number 3:

Traits: Creativity, communication, joy. **Focus:** Expressing yourself creatively and cultivating optimism.

Explanation: As we explore Maturity Number 3, readers will uncover the joy of creative expression and effective communication. This number suggests a focus on cultivating optimism and sharing one's unique creative gifts.

Maturity Number 4:

Traits: Practicality, diligence, organization. **Focus:** Building a solid foundation and working methodically.

Explanation: Maturity Number 4 emphasizes the importance of a structured approach. Readers will learn how practicality, diligence, and organizational skills contribute to building a solid foundation in their later years.

... (Continue in a similar format for each Maturity Number)

Here's a brief overview of the meanings of Maturity Numbers:

1. **Maturity Number 1:**

   - **Traits:** Independence, leadership, assertiveness.

   - **Focus:** Developing self-confidence and taking initiative.

2. **Maturity Number 2:**

   - **Traits:** Cooperation, diplomacy, sensitivity.

   - **Focus:** Nurturing relationships and creating harmony.

3. **Maturity Number 3:**

   - **Traits:** Creativity, communication, joy.

   - **Focus:** Expressing yourself creatively and cultivating optimism.

4. **Maturity Number 4:**

   - **Traits:** Practicality, diligence, organization.

   - **Focus:** Building a solid foundation and working methodically.

5. **Maturity Number 5:**

   - **Traits:** Freedom, adaptability, versatility.

   - **Focus:** Embracing change and exploring new experiences.

6. **Maturity Number 6:**

- **Traits:** Responsibility, compassion, harmony.

- **Focus:** Balancing family and social responsibilities.

7. **Maturity Number 7:**

- **Traits:** Analytical, introspective, spiritual.

- **Focus:** Deepening spiritual understanding and self-reflection.

8. **Maturity Number 8:**

- **Traits:** Ambition, leadership, material success.

- **Focus:** Achieving financial and professional goals.

9. **Maturity Number 9:**

- **Traits:** Compassion, humanitarianism, creativity.

- **Focus:** Contributing to the greater good and embracing universal love.

The maturity number

In numerology, the Maturity Number is one of the core numbers calculated from your birthdate and is believed to represent the traits and characteristics that become more pronounced as you mature. To calculate your Maturity Number, you follow these steps:

1. **Calculate the Expression Number:**

   • Use your full birth name to calculate your Expression Number. This involves assigning numerical values to the letters of your name and adding them up.

2. **Reduce to a Single Digit:**

   • If the result is a two-digit number, reduce it to a single digit by adding the digits together.

3. **Calculate the Soul Urge Number:**

   • Use your vowels in your full birth name to calculate your Soul Urge Number.

4. **Reduce to a Single Digit:**

   • If the result is a two-digit number, reduce it to a single digit by adding the digits together.

5. **Calculate the Maturity Number:**

   • Subtract the reduced Soul Urge Number from the reduced Expression Number.

6. **Reduce to a Single Digit:**

- If the result is a two-digit number, reduce it to a single digit by adding the digits together.

The Maturity Number is associated with the traits and characteristics that become more prominent as you mature and grow older. It provides insights into the aspects of your personality that you are likely to focus on or develop during the later stages of life.

For example, if your Expression Number is 7, your Soul Urge Number is 5, the calculation would be 7 (Expression) - 5 (Soul Urge) = 2 (Maturity Number).

Keep in mind that numerology is a symbolic system, and interpretations may vary. The Maturity Number is just one element in a comprehensive numerological analysis that can provide insights into different aspects of your life and personal development.

How to find and what is my maturity number

To find your Maturity Number in numerology, you need to follow a specific calculation process using your Expression Number and Soul Urge Number. Here are the steps to find and understand your Maturity Number:

1. Calculate Your Expression Number:

- Use your full birth name to calculate your Expression Number. Assign numerical values to each letter in your name using a numerology chart, add them up, and reduce to a single digit. The result is your Expression Number.

2. Calculate Your Soul Urge Number:

- Use the vowels in your full birth name to calculate your Soul Urge Number. Assign numerical values to each vowel, add them up, and reduce to a single digit.

3. Calculate Your Maturity Number:

- Subtract your reduced Soul Urge Number from your reduced Expression Number.

4. Reduce to a Single Digit:

- If the result is a two-digit number, reduce it to a single digit by adding the digits together.

For example, let's say your Expression Number is 7, and your Soul Urge Number is 5:

- Expression Number: 7

- Soul Urge Number: 5

• Maturity Number: 7 - 5 = 2

If the Maturity Number is 2, then you've found your Maturity Number.

5. **Interpret Your Maturity Number:**

• Each number in numerology has specific traits associated with it. Interpret the characteristics of the number you've found as your Maturity Number. For example, a Maturity Number of 2 might suggest a focus on cooperation, harmony, and diplomatic skills as you mature.

Understanding your Maturity Number can provide insights into the traits and characteristics that become more significant in the later stages of your life.

If you'd like to share your Expression Number and Soul Urge Number, I can assist you in calculating your Maturity Number and providing more detailed information based on the specific numbers involved.

Repeating numbers

Introduction: Unveiling the Mystical Language of Repeating Numbers

Step into the enchanting world of numerology as we unravel the hidden significance of repeating numbers. From the intriguing alignment of 111 to the resonating vibrations of 888, each repeated sequence carries a unique and potent message, poised to guide and enlighten those attuned to their ethereal presence.

Understanding the Meanings: Navigating Numerical Insights

Dive into the profound meanings embedded in commonly encountered repeating numbers, exploring their spiritual, emotional, and practical dimensions. This exploration goes beyond simple numerals, providing you, the reader, with profound insights that extend into the depths of self-discovery. Discover how recognizing these recurring numbers can become a transformative tool, fostering self-reflection and creating a deeper connection with the universe.

Practical Applications: Integrating Cosmic Wisdom into Daily Life

This chapter isn't just an exploration; it's a practical guide for seamlessly integrating the awareness of repeating numbers into your everyday existence. Through compelling examples and practical insights, you're encouraged to decipher these symbolic signs, trust your intuition, and embrace the transformative energies woven into each number. It's a roadmap for incorporating numerological wisdom into the fabric of your daily life.

Case Studies and Testimonials: Stories of Cosmic Connection

Immerse yourself in real-life narratives that traverse the realms of repeating numbers. Through case studies and heartfelt testimonials, witness the profound impact these numerical messages have had on lives. This personal touch not only adds authenticity but serves as a testament to the profound influence that the hidden language of numbers can wield.

Conclusion: Harmonizing with the Cosmic Symphony

As you conclude this chapter, you'll emerge with a newfound appreciation for the symphony of the hidden language of repeating numbers. Whether perceived as a comforting presence, a beckoning call to action, or a guiding light in times of uncertainty, these numerical sequences transcend mere digits. They become a source of inspiration, a conduit to cosmic connection, and a reminder of the divine forces that intricately surround and shape your journey.

By seamlessly incorporating this rich tapestry of information into your reading experience, you'll gain not only a guide but a profound understanding of the mystical meanings embedded in the repetition of numbers. It's an invitation to embark on a transformative exploration, unlocking the secrets of the numerical universe and fostering a deeper connection with the cosmic energies that dance through your life.

In the context of numerology, repeating numbers are often considered as powerful and meaningful symbols. Many people believe that when they consistently encounter the same number sequence, such as 111, 222, 333, and so on, it holds special significance. Here's a general overview of the meanings associated with some commonly encountered repeating numbers:

Repeating Numbers in Numerology

111:

Meaning: New beginnings, alignment, and spiritual awakening. Pay attention to your thoughts and intentions.

222:

Meaning: Harmony, balance, and partnerships. It suggests that everything is in divine order.

333:

Meaning: Divine protection and guidance. It signifies the presence of angels and ascended masters.

444:

Meaning: Protection and support from your angels. A sign that they are near and assisting you.

555:

Meaning: Change is coming. Embrace the transformation and be open to new opportunities.

666:

Meaning: Often associated with negative connotations, but it can also represent balance between the material and spiritual aspects of life.

777:

Meaning: A sign of divine intervention and spiritual awareness. Trust your intuition and spiritual path.

888:

Meaning: Abundance and financial prosperity. It suggests that you are on the right path.

999:

Meaning: Completion and a time for wrapping up old chapters. It may indicate the end of a cycle.

000:

Meaning: A fresh start or a blank slate. It symbolizes infinite potential and the beginning of a spiritual journey.

IN CONCLUSION, NUMEROLOGY is a fascinating tool for self-discovery, offering insights into your inherent traits, tendencies, and potential challenges. By understanding your Life Path, Expression, and Soul Urge Numbers, you gain a unique perspective on various aspects of your life, from career choices to relationships.

It's important to debunk common myths about numerology, clarifying that it's not about predicting the future or wielding mystical powers. Instead, numerology is a symbolic and methodical system that has ancient roots and is accessible to anyone interested in exploring it.

Numerology can be integrated into daily rituals and decision-making processes, providing a mindful and intentional approach to life. Whether it's aligning with your Life Path in the morning, choosing numerologically favorable dates, or reflecting on your Soul Urge in the evening, numerology offers practical insights for personal growth.

Encouraging readers to explore numerology for personal growth, it's a tool that complements other self-awareness practices. By incorporating numerology into daily life, individuals can deepen their understanding of themselves, make informed choices, and cultivate a more fulfilling and aligned existence. Embrace numerology as a guide on your journey of self-discovery, unlocking the potential for personal growth and a richer, more conscious life.

Conclusion

Alright, so here we are, wrapping up our exploration of the "Numerology 101 Beginner's Guide to Numerology." Throughout our journey together, we've delved into the intricate world of numerology, uncovering the mysteries behind numbers and their profound impact on our lives.

In these pages, we've decoded the secrets of life paths, destiny numbers, and the significance of each digit. The essence of numerology has been demystified, making it accessible and engaging for everyone, regardless of prior knowledge.

As we bid adieu to this insightful adventure, take with you the understanding that numbers are more than just symbols – they hold the keys to self-discovery and empowerment. From deciphering your personal numbers to embracing the magic within them, the "Numerology 101 Beginner's Guide to Numerology" has been a guide, a companion in your journey to unlock the secrets of your own story.

So, as you close the book, carry the wisdom of numerology with you. Let the revelations within these pages be a source of inspiration and guidance in your daily life. May the numbers continue to whisper their secrets, guiding you on a path of self-discovery and personal growth. Cheers to the magic of numbers and the endless possibilities they unveil!

Contact the astrologer
Dear Reader

WE EXTEND OUR SINCERE thanks to you, dear readers, for embarking on this astrological journey with us. Your curiosity, engagement, and trust have made this exploration of the Zodiac sign Cancer all the more fulfilling.

In these pages, we have delved into the essence of the Cancer sign, unveiling its secrets, traits, and the horoscope for 2024. We've ventured through the depths of emotion, explored the intricacies of relationships, and discovered the likes and dislikes of a Cancer individual. All of this would not have been possible without your interest and presence.

Your quest for knowledge and self-discovery is what fuels our passion for astrology, and we are grateful to have been your guides in this cosmic voyage. We hope that the insights and wisdom shared in these pages serve as a guiding light in your life.

We invite you to explore our other books, each dedicated to a unique Zodiac sign and various aspects of astrology. Whether you seek to deepen your understanding of the stars or uncover the mysteries of other signs, you'll find a wealth of knowledge waiting for you.

Should you have any questions, insights, or simply wish to connect with us, please don't hesitate to reach out.

You can contact us via **WhatsApp at +1 829-205-5456** or **email us at danielsanjurjo47@gmail.com.**

May the stars continue to shine brightly on your path, and may your journey through the Zodiac signs be filled with enlightenment, growth, and harmony. **Sincerely Daniel Sanjurjo**

About the Author

Daniel Sanjurjo is a passionate author who delves into the realms of astrology and self-help. With a gift for exploring the celestial and the human psyche, Daniel's books are celestial journeys of self-discovery and personal growth. Join the cosmic odyssey with this insightful writer.

Don't miss out!

Visit the website below and you can sign up to receive emails whenever Daniel Sanjurjo publishes a new book. There's no charge and no obligation.

https://books2read.com/r/B-A-WQHBB-TYBTC

Did you love *Numerology 101 Beginner's Guide to Numerology*? Then you should read *Dreams Interpretation Guide*[1] by Daniel Sanjurjo!

[2]

◈ Unlock the Secrets of Dreams with "Dreamscape Chronicles: A Journey into the World of Dreams"

◈ Are you ready to embark on a profound dream interpretation journey that will unveil the hidden meanings of your dreams, offering insights into your inner self, personal growth, and self-discovery? "Dreamscape Chronicles" is your definitive guide to navigating the enigmatic landscapes of the subconscious mind.

◈ Explore the Depths of Dream Analysis: Delve into the intricate world of dream interpretation, where the symbols and stories of the night come alive. From common dreams to the mysteries of the mind, this book unravels the symbolism and significance of your dreamscapes.

◈ Illuminate Your Path: Discover how dreams can inspire your creativity, provide therapeutic insights, and awaken your inner desires. This book serves as

---

1. https://books2read.com/u/38Ykxd

2. https://books2read.com/u/38Ykxd

your compass, guiding you through the rich tapestry of dreams and helping you harness their potential.

◈ Key Topics Explored: Uncover the significance of dream symbolism, the role of common dream themes, and the influence of pioneers like Sigmund Freud in understanding the profound landscapes of the dreamer's mind.

Are you ready to embark on a journey through the dreamer's world? "Dreamscape Chronicles" is your passport to the boundless landscapes of your own mind. Explore, interpret, and awaken to the possibilities hidden within your dreams.

Unlock the mysteries of your dreams and start your journey of self-discovery today!

Also by Daniel Sanjurjo

Birthdays Profiles
The Secret Language of Birthdays Profiles - January Personality Insights.
The Secret Language of Birthdays - February Personality Insights
The Secret Language of Birthdays March Profiles

Zodiaco
Aries 2024 Mes Por Mes
Tauro 2024 Mes Por Mes
Géminis 2024 Mes Por Mes
Cáncer 2024 Mes Por Mes
Leo 2024 Mes Por Mes:
Virgo 2024 Mes Por Mes
Libra 2024 Mes Por Mes
Escorpio 2024 Mes Por Mes
Sagitario 2024 Mes Por Mes
Capricornio 2024 Mes Por Mes
Acuario 2024 Mes Por Mes
Piscis 2024: Un Viaje Celestial
Piscis 2024 Mes Por Mes

Zodiac world
Aries Revealed 2024

Taurus 2024
Leo 2024
Gemini 2024
Cancer horoscope 2024
Virgo 2024
Scorpio 2024
Sagittarius 2024
Capricorn 2024
Aquarius 2024

Standalone
Cosmic Revelations 2024
Dreams Interpretation Guide
Explorando Mis Sueños: Descubre el Mundo Fascinante de tu Mente Nocturna
Moon And Astrology Planner 2024
Numerology 101 Beginner's Guide to Numerology